Introduction

We live in an era of unprecedented stress on our planet. The combination of population growth, climate change, resource demand, and the continuing development of coastal and built areas creates significant challenges for the Nation. To meet these challenges, there is a need for information about the Earth system and how it is changing over time. A robust infrastructure of Earth observations is necessary to support the Nation's need to inform decisions and policy. Additionally, in this ever more global society, information and understanding derived from Earth observations are important in sustaining the U.S. role in global leadership.

The U.S. Government recognizes that a coordinated approach is needed to sustain and build on the current set of Earth observations. Beyond coordination, there is a need for a continued national commitment to ensure that Earth observations, like other critical infrastructure, are maintained and continued.

What's at Stake

OUR WELFARE AND OUR PRODUCTIVITY:
CLIMATE AND ENERGY

Global climate change presents us with a complex and inextricably-linked mix of environmental, economic, security, and political issues for all nations on the planet. It is a long-term, century-to-millennial problem, the outcomes of which directly depend on the soundness of decisions being made today. Climate change is most clearly defined at the global scale. However, society faces greater challenges in characterizing, understanding, and predicting its impacts at the scale of local communities and individuals. Decisions being made over such an unprecedented range of temporal and geographic scales, and affecting all human activity, must rest on the bedrock of accurate scientific information. This information must be derived from comprehensive, coordinated, and sustained observations of the Earth system in order to characterize the impacts of climate change, and inform our plans for adaptation and mitigation.

We see extraordinary changes in Alaska, Greenland, the Arctic, and Antarctica, with loss of permafrost, glacial mass and sea ice, as well as rising sea levels and coastal erosion, all occurring faster than previously projected. The oceans are acidifying, likely due to rising atmospheric CO_2 levels, with potentially catastrophic consequences for fisheries and coral reefs. These changes have implications for a host of activities such as shipping, resource development, fishing, tourism, subsistence livelihoods, ecosystem health, and scientific exploration, as well as creating new national and economic security concerns. Gaps in our ability to observe and track these changes will lead to deficiencies in our ability to better understand and project future change and to better craft our near- and long-term response.

Energy is essential to increasing standards of living around the world and is the root of our climate change challenge. The widespread and large-scale use of fossil fuels such as coal, gas, and oil is the primary contributor to increases in greenhouse gas concentrations. Expected increases in world population, together with the desire for economic development, guarantee a growing demand for energy. The extent to which fossil fuels and other energy sources continue to be used will determine the future human influence on the global climate, and whether the rapid increase in greenhouse gas concentrations will continue during this century. Managing the risks of climate change will require a profound, systematic, and global transformation in the production and consumption of energy. Observations of natural resources such as wind, water, and sunlight are essential to manage current and future renewable energy technologies effectively and to deploy the "smart" electrical grid needed to improve the efficiency, reliability, and flexibility of electricity production and consumption.

If the nations of the world were to limit the use of fossil fuels, the right to emit carbon dioxide could become an increasingly valuable traded commodity. In such a world, observations of the location, amount, and rate of carbon dioxide emission into the air, as well as the stock and flow of all forms of carbon on land and in the oceans, will be needed to manage a global carbon market fairly and efficiently. Finally, we need observations to characterize the location, magnitude, and rate of climate change impacts to strike an ongoing balance between investments in adaptation, and building the new energy infrastructure and systems for a sustainable future.

LIFE ON EARTH:
NATURE, FOOD, WATER AND HEALTH

Human existence depends on the thin layer that is the biosphere—a system that is being increasingly stressed, modified, and simplified by human activities. These changes are increasing species extinctions and reducing the resiliency and long-term capacity of biological systems to respond to change and produce the goods and services upon which we depend. The global population will likely reach 9 billion by 2050, and providing the food, goods, and services for such a population will necessitate changes in many areas. A rising standard of living in countries such as China, India, and Brazil, as well as the diversion of some food crops to ethanol production, have put increased pressure on current food production and distribution systems. Over-fishing and degradation of coastal and marine ecosystems are putting further pressure on providing nutrition to the people of the world. Food security is a major issue that can lead to the fall of governments, human suffering, political instability, and human migration.

The 2008 U.S. National Defense Strategy identified population growth and competition for scarce resources as key security challenges facing our Nation, and the 2005 Millennium Ecosystem Assessment showed how many of the ecosystem services upon which we depend are being degraded globally and/or locally.[3] Over 20 percent of the global population relies on ocean fisheries and aquaculture as their primary source of protein. However, overexploitation of many fish stocks and alteration of habitats due to human activities and/or natural influences such as climate change have already had profound consequences for many ecosystems and fishing communities.[4] In addition to the security of our food, our welfare is also inextricably linked to air and water quality and increasing ocean acidification.

Air pollution in the lower troposphere is a major factor in cardiovascular and respiratory disease. By U.S. air quality standards, one-third of the U.S. population lives in counties or parishes that do not meet national air quality standards.[5] Particulate pollution and tropospheric ozone, the principal components of photochemical smog, are also significant factors that influence climate. The National Research Council (NRC) has questioned whether current air quality monitoring infrastructure is adequate to meet the challenges of air quality management over the next several decades.[6] While the integration of remote sensing observations with *in situ* data promises to deliver greater understanding of air pollution, ambient monitoring of air quality at the surface, where exposure to pollution occurs, will continue to be an essential component of the Nation's Earth observation system. Air pollution quickly crosses political boundaries, so an effective monitoring network needs to be able to integrate observations collected by different agencies and governments at Federal, state, and local levels.

The Nation's water supply is also of paramount importance to economic development, food production, and recreation. Severe drought over the last few years has struck parts of the West and Southwest where population growth is among the Nation's most rapid, and in many parts of the country aquifers are being drawn down at rates greater than the rate at which they are being replenished. High levels of suspended solids and sediments transport nutrients, other organic matter, and contaminants and can degrade the quality of receiving waters and damage the downstream ecosystems, as evidenced by the existence of hypoxia zones in areas of river discharge. Sediments also create infrastructure problems by filling in dams and creating conditions for seasonal flooding.

The U.S. has invested enormous resources in the development and maintenance of water infrastructure. Unfortunately, much of this infrastructure is aging and was constructed in a time that could not have predicted the current competition for water. Finally, due to political and bureaucratic boundaries, water monitoring is not organized on a regional or continental scale with any uniformity, adding to the challenge of providing a comprehensive solution.

It has been known for some years now that the oceans of the world are carbon sinks—absorbing about 30 percent of the carbon dioxide released from the burning of fossil fuels, thus reducing the atmospheric carbon.[7] While this is beneficial in terms of global warming concerns, research has shown that this is resulting in chemical processes which are making the oceans more acidic. Ocean acidification has enormous implications for biodiversity and ecosystems, resulting in the degradation of coral reefs, stresses to the metabolic rates of many species, and declining reproductive health of oceanic organisms. This phenomenon will have major impacts on human health and well-being as so much of the world is dependent on the resources of the reefs and ocean waters for food, recreation, tourism, and coastal protection. Additional research and monitoring is needed to expand our understanding of these issues and correctly build them into management and climate models. While the oceans provide resources critical to human survival and well-being, they also can pose risks, including exposure to aquatic toxins and pathogens. Observations are central to providing timely and accurate measurements of waterborne pathogens, toxic algae, and other toxins.

Infectious disease already contributes to over twenty five percent of global deaths. Climate change—such as warmer temperatures, changes in rainfall patterns, and reduced freezes—means that disease vectors carrying diseases such as West Nile virus, Hanta viruses, malaria and dengue fever (i.e., mosquitoes, rodents and other mammals) will be able to exist in areas where they have not previously been or in higher numbers, causing more illness and challenges for our public health surveillance and response systems.

OUR LIVES AND PROPERTY:
DISASTERS AND EXTREME WEATHER

Each year in the U.S., natural hazards cause hundreds of deaths and cost billions of dollars in disaster response, disruption of commerce, and destruction of homes and critical infrastructure. Although the number of lives lost to natural hazards each year has generally declined, the economic cost of major disaster response and recovery continues to rise, in part because of growing populations and investments in coastal and other vulnerable areas. In each recent decade, property damage from natural hazard events has doubled or tripled. Today, the U.S. ranks second only to Japan in economic damages resulting from natural disasters. Improved Earth observations help reduce disaster losses by increasing the scientific understanding of why, where, how, and when natural disasters occur, characterizing natural hazards and their risks, using natural and human infrastructure to minimize impact, and detecting and tracking hazardous phenomena through monitoring networks, improved disaster response policies, and implementation.

Coastal storms alone cost the U.S. roughly $7 billion per year.[8] Sustained Earth observations enable us to build complex models of hurricanes, providing better prediction, response, and planning for future development to minimize damage and loss of life and infrastructure. Continuity of meteorological data is essential to storm prediction; delays in planned meteorological satellites could have major impacts on our ability to predict and monitor the path and intensity of tropical storms.

At the same time, the Nation experiences thousands of earthquakes annually, with an average of seven large enough to cause serious damage.[9] Seventy-five million Americans in 39 states face significant risk from earthquakes, which hold the potential to deliver devastating blows to urban areas across the country with projected losses up to a quarter-trillion dollars from a single event.[10] In addition to strong earth shaking from the main shock and aftershocks, earthquakes can produce devastating secondary effects such as fires, landslides, liquefaction, floods, and tsunamis.

Before the introduction of controlled burning, decades of efforts directed at extinguishing every fire that burned on public lands seriously disrupted the natural role of fire in many of our Nation's most vital ecosystems. In recent years, total lands burned have increased significantly, nearly doubling the area burned 20 years ago.[11] Data from satellites, manned and unmanned aerial vehicles, and ground-based sensors that are critical for national and state fire management are not adequate to ensure preparedness for wildland fire management and ecosystem restoration.

In 2003 alone, wildfires in Southern California claimed 22 lives and destroyed 3,600 homes.[12] Generally these homes were located in areas "where structures and other human development meet or intermingle with undeveloped wildland or vegetative fuels."[13] Development in the wildland-urban interface continues to grow. In the Western U.S. alone, 38 percent of new home construction is adjacent to or intermixed with the wildland/urban interface.[14] In the face of this growing challenge, an important tool for detecting and monitoring wildland fires could degrade in the near future with the likely loss of key satellite instruments.

Our ability to monitor the vitality of our planet and its productivity is critical to manage our environment, food, water and health, and to protect our lives and property. In each of these areas, Earth observations currently supply information for decision making, and today, some measurements are incomplete, either in coverage, periodicity, or length of time series. This limits our potential for understanding, modeling, and forecasting. Prioritizing measurements and improving the coordination of our Earth observing systems would help prepare the Nation to meet the challenges of the future.

What's Needed

Physical, chemical, and biological information about our planet is vital to our ability to plan, predict, respond, and to protect our citizens and infrastructure. Today, millions of individual observations are collected every day, allowing us to examine, monitor, and try to model atmospheric composition, seismic activity, ecosystem health, weather patterns, and hundreds of other characteristics of our planet.

Observations are taken from space, and within the Earth system (*in situ*), from the air, in the water, and on and below the land and the oceans. They are measured by sensors and by people. The data they provide are interpreted, interpolated, and integrated. The myriad of observations taken today vary widely in purpose and scope and are appropriately distributed among hundreds of programs under the purview of Federal agencies and other institutions and individuals. To a large degree, these observations have been only loosely coupled, coordinated, and integrated, although there are notable exceptions such as the Global Energy and Water Cycle Experiment (GEWEX). GEWEX successfully integrates activities both nationally and internationally to better observe, understand, and model the hydrological cycle and energy fluxes in the Earth's atmosphere and at the surface, providing a great example of what can be done. The leap forward can only be achieved with a synergy between remotely sensed and *in situ* observations supported by robust, interoperable data systems that allow for long-term access and archive as well as the opportunity for long term monitoring and assessment of status and trends.

Increasingly this promise is being realized, and seemingly disparate observations are combined in new ways to produce benefits across multiple societal areas. This recognition has led to the concept of an integrated Earth observing system as articulated by the U.S. Group on Earth Observations (USGEO).[15] In order to achieve the synergies and benefits of an integrated system of observations, USGEO identified the following needed elements.

1) A sustainable observing system of systems that focuses on enabling useful products for decision-makers and is achieved through a flexible, yet disciplined approach in coordination with all partners;

2) Data systems that utilize common data formats and information protocols for easy, timely, information sharing and system interoperability; and

3) Quality-control systems that ensure accurate, long-term data records for important environmental and climate parameters.

These elements collectively form the basis of the Global Earth Observation System of Systems (GEOSS), a multinational effort working to realize a future wherein decisions and actions are informed by coordinated, comprehensive, and sustained Earth observations and information.

This assessment reaffirms the importance of these three overarching elements to the realization of maximum benefits from Earth observations. While there are issues and concerns with all of the components, this assessment focuses on the first element, the resource-intensive observational component.

The identification of observations needed derives from a consideration of societal, economic, regulatory, and scientific imperatives. Table 1 shows a limited cross section of observational parameters and their scientific and operational contributions across the "What's at Stake" themes. This Table is not comprehensive and is intended only to be illustrative of the variety of benefits gained from selected observations. Even a cursory analysis with respect to societal benefits reveals that synergies among the observable parameters argue strongly for a balanced approach to system configuration. In the balanced approach, emphasis is given to obtaining as many of the observable parameters as possible, rather than extensive measurement of only a few parameters.

Table 1. Crosscutting Applications of Selected Earth Observations

	Climate and Energy	Nature, Food, Water and Health	Disasters and Extreme Weather
Precipitation	Climate variability Available water-cooling capacity for energy production	Agricultural productivity Disease vector predictions Flooding Drinking water availability Global water cycle Sustainable development Ecosystem health	Flooding Coastal innundation Landslides Weather forecasting
Vegetation	Anthropogenic impacts to climate Global carbon cycle Sea ice, glaciation and snow pack assessment Sunlight interaction with vegetated surfaces Biofuel production, energy exploration Energy resource assessment Ecosystem characterization Land use change, landscape ecology Habitat and wetlands management and ecological forecasting	Monitoring crops, deforestation Famine prediction Foreign agricultural assessment Global food security Disease vector growth Evaporation, Transpiration Water drainage prediction Snow accumulation and melt Water resource assessment and management Salinization	Water drainage predictions for flooding Disaster mitigation and response Coastal zone assessment and monitoring
Soil Moisture	Monitoring areas of desertification Land use change and impact on climate	Crop yield predictions Drought analysis Irrigation management Infectious disease vector growth Food production Plant and animal growth Key element of water cycle Freeze-thaw state	Flooding and wildfire potential Improved model of surface and atmospheric interaction, evaporation rates Initialization of weather models Evaporation/transpiration rates
Ecosystems and Biodiversity	Monitoring effects of climate change Quantification and characterization of ecosystems Ecosystem health Carbon sequestration Biofuels	Plant and animal important to food production and yield (honey bees, pests, invasive species, etc.) Ecosystem role in replenishing clean water Sustainment of fisheries Pharmaceutical discoveries Development and spread of new or re-emerging diseases	Land use/land change inputs to models Surface/atmosphere interaction Protection from coastal storms Erosion, landslides, etc. Flooding

What Can Be Achieved

The coupling of diverse observations has revolutionized such areas as weather forecasting, environmental monitoring, and the projection of stratospheric ozone depletion. Such coupling holds great promise for many other applications such as the monitoring of our Nation's forests and predicting disease outbreaks around the world.

Dramatic improvements in our ability to forecast the weather began in the 1960s with the advent of the first geostationary and polar-orbiting satellites that could deliver weather information from space. Since that time, satellite observations have been complemented with surface-based Doppler weather radars, radiosondes that gather atmospheric profiles, and a network of human and automated surface *in situ* observations that continuously collect weather data. Additional systems are under development to further improve weather forecasting, such as the implementation of phased array radar technology, which has the potential to boost tornado warning lead times from 10-15 minutes to 45 minutes. Integration of data available from a wide variety of sources, governmental and non-governmental, creating regional or local "mesonets" also have the potential to boost forecast accuracy on a finer scale than is currently possible.[16] Over the same period, the world scientific community, through the World Meteorological Organization (WMO), established an unparalleled data collection and distribution framework that allows all users worldwide free access to weather data, greatly improving weather models and weather prediction.

Ozone depletion projections followed a similar path of progress. Originally developed for weather applications, satellite sensors of backscattered solar ultraviolet light were found to provide critical measures of total ozone column. When ground-based sensors revealed in 1986 that dramatic ozone depletion was occurring in the springtime Antarctic stratosphere, satellite sensors were able to verify the loss and measure its geographic extent. Observations of ozone-destroying chemicals by other satellite and aircraft instruments quickly led to a revolution in our understanding of ozone chemistry. The new ozone depletion picture provided a sound basis for eventual international agreements limiting the use of chlorofluorocarbons.

Scientists are beginning to use satellite imagery to identify the climatic conditions that drive the emergence of infectious diseases or their vectors. This is being done for diseases such as cholera, Chikungunya fever, Rift Valley fever, dengue fever, West Nile virus, Hanta virus, and Ebola River hemoragghic fever.[17] As more links between Earth observations and human health are confirmed, the opportunity to assess and manage those risks will increase. These links can only be proven and expanded by the long-term availability of ground-based and remote sensing data that reveal patterns or trends that allow more accurate forecasting.

Not all important phenomena can be observed from space or in the atmosphere. While primary carbon production of the world's oceans and forests can be measured from satellites, many details below the surfaces require *in situ* measurements. In the ocean, observation of biodiversity requires sustained sampling and observing from ships with deployment of traditional and novel technologies such as acoustics, remote vehicles, and tracking networks. These observations are necessary to support ecosystem-based management rather than single species or issue-by-issue approaches. Similarly, terrestrial systems need a range of instrumented and human-mediated sampling and observations to measure the key components of the environment.

We can expect future observations to yield a profusion of beneficial applications from confronting climate change, to improving human health, sustaining food and water supplies, and protecting against natural disasters. In all cases, the key to achieving benefits will be sustaining strategic investments in observational capabilities.

Where We Are Now

The state of U.S.-led Earth observations was documented in the 2005 Strategic Plan for the U.S. Integrated Earth Observation System (IEOS). The IEOS plan described an overall system with broad, but uneven effectiveness across nine identified societal benefits (Figure 1). This list is not in order of priority, nor is it meant to be exhaustive or static. On one end of the spectrum, weather observations, which are supported by roughly half of the Federal investment in Earth observations, were recognized to form the most mature system. At the other end of the spectrum, an integrated climate observing system was far from mature, with very few of its measurement components achieving a large temporal span or spatial distribution. Observational issues were identified for each of the benefit areas; chief among them were the continuity of key measurements and the development of new, transformational observations.

The state of the U.S. space-based observational system in 2009 was largely unchanged from that of 2005, when an interim report of the National Research Council's committee that produced the Earth Science and Applications from Space "Decadal Survey" Report described the national system of environmental satellites as "at risk of collapse." Later, in 2007, the Decadal Survey Report concluded the outlook had significantly worsened. The likelihood of a degradation in land imagery capability, affecting multiple societal needs (e.g., agriculture, biodiversity, climate, ecosystems, water, etc.), was almost a certainty. In addition, no plans had been developed to continue some of the valuable observations demonstrated by the NASA Earth Observing System (EOS) program that benefit the disaster preparedness, human health, climate, and water areas. Continuity of the weather observing system was also threatened by reductions and delays in the National Polar-Orbiting Operational Environmental Satellite System (NPOESS) program.

As of FY 2010, deployments of new and replacement satellites are still not keeping pace with the termination of older systems, even though many existing satellites are operating well past their nominal lifetimes. A number of satellites built as research missions were seen to have ongoing societal benefit, but there were no plans for continuity of many of these. Given the long development times associated with fielding new systems, particularly satellite systems, a sustained commitment to sensor system development is necessary to avoid a loss of observing capability in the next decade.

For example, the Landsat series of satellites has provided images of the Earth's land surface for over 38 years, but the future availability of this imagery from the existing Landsat satellites remains uncertain. Although Landsats 5 and 7 are currently on-orbit, Landsat 5 was launched in 1984 and has far exceeded its expected life, while Landsat 7 has developed a technical anomaly that limits the utility of its imagery. NASA and the U.S. Geological Survey (USGS) are developing the Landsat Data Continuity Mission (LDCM) with a planned launch in late 2012. Planning for future Landsat missions is being undertaken by the USGS and NASA, in cooperation with other stakeholders.

For the ocean, ocean color data have proved to be a key climate variable in quantifying carbon uptake from the atmosphere by phytoplankton in addition to understanding the impacts of global warming on ocean ecological systems.[18] The Sea-viewing Wide Field-of-view Sensor (SeaWiFS) satellite has provided 13 years of near-continuous observation of oceanic primary production since its launch on August 1, 1997. However, the satellite system is far past its operational life expectancy. The Moderate Resolution Imaging Spectroradiometer (MODIS) instrument on NASA's Aqua satellite, which also provides ocean color data, is also past its nominal lifetime. Significant delays in the NPOESS program, and continued uncertainty as to how well the ocean color sensor on the NPOESS Preparatory Project (NPP) will be able to provide continuity for the SeaWiFS data record, leave the U.S. without clear continuity of certain satellite-based oceanic primary productivity estimates. In the near term, NOAA and NASA are actively pursuing international partnerships with agencies such as the European Space Agency (ESA), the Japan Aerospace Exploration Agency (JAXA), and the Indian Space Research Organization (ISRO), which have satellites (current and planned) that may help to mitigate this potential gap. On February 1, 2010, the Administration announced that the NPOESS program would be restructured. NOAA will be responsible for the afternoon orbit with the Joint Polar Satellite System (JPSS) and the Department of Defense will be responsible for the early morning orbit with the Defense Weather Satellite System. The JPSS satellite is intended to provide continuity of measurements that had been planned for the afternoon orbit of the NPOESS program including ocean color measurements.

- Improve Weather Forecasting
- Reduce Loss of Life and Property from Disasters
- Protect and Monitor our Ocean Resource
- Understand, Assess, Predict, Mitigate, and Adapt to Climate Variability and Change
- Support Sustainable Agriculture and Forestry, and Combat Land Degradation
- Understand the Effect of Environmental Factors on Human Health and Well-Being
- Develop the Capacity to make Ecological Forecasts
- Protect and Monitor Water Resources
- Monitor and Manage Energy Resources

Figure 1. USGEO Societal Benefits

Development of an integrated climate observing system continues to stand as a large and urgent challenge.[19] One part of the challenge is that the required observing system must deliver multi-decade data records with the accuracy and precision needed to distinguish long-term climate changes from natural variability and other environmental influences.

Two examples of high precision multi-decade data records are the Department of Energy's Atmospheric Radiation Measurement (ARM) Climate Research Facility and the NASA Earth Observing System (EOS). The three fixed ARM sites represent ground and aerial measurements and have been measuring clouds, aerosols, and radiation in different climatic regimes for over a decade. These data are available to the general science community in near real time. EOS demonstrated the ability to create long-term, high-precision satellite climate data records. Diagnosing systematic biases and bridging unintentional gaps in long-term records are ever-present challenges to successful implementation of a climate observing system for both space- or ground-based measurements.

The EOS accomplishments revealed many of the difficulties in "transitioning" long-term, research-type measurements to an operational system. Understanding and correcting for such measurement challenges requires researchers and specialists who are intimately familiar with the instrument technology, and are dedicated to data integrity and uncovering the workings of the Earth system. Owing to these challenges, the distinction between "research" and "operational" capabilities and assets must be considered in order to successfully deliver sustained climate-related measurements. Accordingly, overcoming the limitations of the current "research to operations" paradigm with respect to climate observations, which require a long-term research effort, requires more formal attention. The institutional structures and capacity, and agency roles and responsibilities must be developed to deliver an integrated climate observing system.

In a world of limited resources, sound stewardship and international collaboration are also of great importance in the realm of satellites. In the past, nations and agencies focused internally on needs to meet individual missions utilizing agency-centric requirements processes. However, the high cost of replacing and expanding observing infrastructure, coupled with difficulty in addressing key data gaps as well as data continuity has brought greater visibility to the fact that nations and agencies can no longer go it alone. There is a pressing need to leverage national and international contributions as well as those from industry and academia to share costs, eliminate duplication of effort, and increase our ability to cover gaps. This includes observing infrastructure as well as our ability to obtain access to and leverage data from relevant foreign sources. The intergovernmental Group on Earth Observations (GEO), the international Committee on Earth Observation Satellites (CEOS), the U.S. Group on Earth Observations (USGEO), and many other important groups have been established to enhance this collaboration. These organizations can serve as a force multiplier, allowing partners to capitalize on each others' strengths in fostering the common good.

The Assessment Process and Priorities

In June 2008 the USGEO Strategic Assessment Group (SAG) began to develop its first set of recommendations for national Earth observation priorities. The charge to the group was unique in that the focus was not only to be across all U.S. government agencies and the nine USEGO societal benefit areas, but also was to include measurements from all types of platforms: space-based, land and sea-based, airborne, subsurface, and observations collected by humans.

The initial step in this assessment was for the societal benefit area subgroups to comprehensively gather the key observations identified by national and international panels of experts. This resulted in a large number of measurements. The team then focused on measurements that had multiple benefits across the Societal Benefit Areas (SBAs) or measurements that were deemed critical to an individual SBA. This greatly narrowed the set of observations being assessed. In the next step the team evaluated each measurement in terms of whether it was particularly at risk, with a current or looming gap in a valuable data record, or was an observation that is not yet being made but held great promise for providing dramatic gains or a scientific breakthrough. This resulted in 17 specific observations. Finally, the team considered additional observing components that either serve as necessary enablers of the 17, or allowed greater opportunity for exploitation of a particular measurement. This step ensured that important calibration and reference measurements were included, as well as adding greater spatial resolution or providing the potential for greater understanding and interpretation of results. A schematic of this process is shown in Figure 2. The resulting priority observations are listed alphabetically in Table 2, and greater detail for each can be found in the supplement at the end of the document. Though not the focus of this assessment, the SAG also strongly noted the need for effective data management systems to provide access, quality control, and archiving to maximize usefulness of all observations.

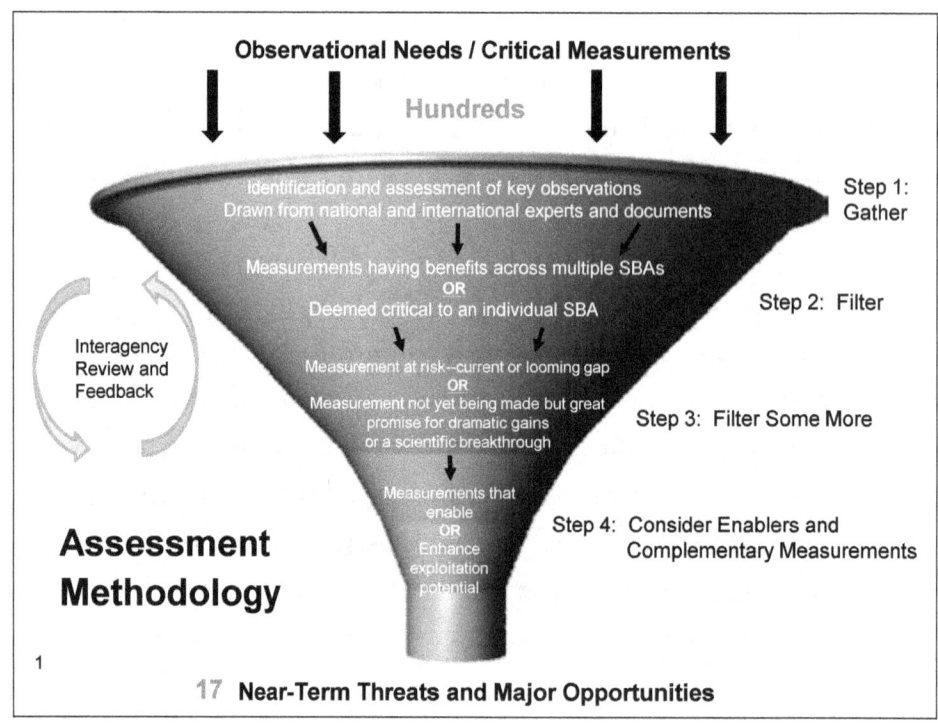

Figure 2. Assessment Methodology

In completing this assessment, the SAG assumed that some systems funded and currently under development, such as the NPOESS Preparatory Project (NPP), JPSS and the Geostationary Operational Environmental Satellite R-Series (GOES-R) will be successfully put into operation. Aside from observations to support weather forecasting, a few climate-related parameters, and the single Landsat data continuity mission scheduled for late 2012, there were few definite plans for sustained measurements of many other critical observable parameters until the FY2011 Budget. Some of the current measurement series that have been collected through successive research efforts are recognized to be under immediate threat of discontinuity. At the same time, some shorter-term measurement series are increasingly earning recognition as scientifically important and as being candidates for longer sustained collection.

Individual agencies are confronted with maintaining and improving existent systems and developing new systems within a difficult fiscal environment. In addition, there is increasing recognition for the need to define a new structure for sustained Earth observing systems, particularly for climate, in a way that addresses the need for highly accurate and precise long-term data records. The need for a more comprehensive understanding of global carbon and its fluxes between the atmospheric, terrestrial, and oceanic reservoirs is paramount. While not called out as a single comprehensive priority in Table 2, the elements of a global carbon observing system are contained within the priorities for greenhouse gases, landscape characterization / vegetation, and ocean color.

Achieving benefits in the nine societal benefit areas defined by USGEO requires more than integrating observation and monitoring into a coordinated system. It requires a broader scheme that includes models to process data, to simulate phenomena, and to forecast conditions as well as the data centers, scientists, and systems of data curation to leverage past, present, and future expenditures most effectively, and tools to provide a useful interface for decision makers. To move forward, the SAG recommended establishing collective near-term priorities such as those documented in Table 2 of this document to help the U.S. Government sustain and improve key Earth observations.

Building on the recommendations presented by the SAG, OSTP articulates in this report a preliminary plan for achieving and sustaining U.S.-based Earth observations. Table 2 and the supplement highlight recent investments during the Obama Administration through 2009, including the American Recovery and Reinvestment Act of 2009 and 2010 appropriations to implement many of the priorities outlined in the strategic assessment. Table 2 and the supplement also highlight proposed investments in the President's 2011 Budget to achieve and sustain Earth observations.

We are Making Progress

The Administration has taken decisive steps to begin reversing the trend of declining observational capabilities. The longer term need is the development of an overall national strategy for Earth observations.

The initial step was to put the Nation's system of polar-orbiting operational environmental satellites on a path to success, as plans for continuity of a number of Earth observations from space had been tied to NPOESS at one point or another in the program's history. There was first a need to "bound" the capabilities of the polar-orbiting operational environmental satellites in order to avoid the problem of having large, monolithic platforms responsible for obtaining an overly broad set of measurements, which contributed to the fragility of the constellation of Earth observing satellites by having a "single string" failure mode. Once the "bounds" of the future platforms were determined, only then could the Administration focus on where the agencies needed "to fill in the gaps" in terms of continuity of key climate observations.

For the near-term, the Administration has recently taken a significant step in regards to continuity of key weather and climate data from space with the decision to restructure the NPOESS program with revised agency responsibilities for implementation of observational assets. NOAA was assigned responsibility for the afternoon orbit and for fielding of the shared ground system. The NOAA JPSS will support this effort by delivering observations in the afternoon orbit. The Department of Defense (DOD) was assigned responsibility for the early morning orbit. Responsibility for the mid-morning observations remains unchanged, and will be provided by the European Organisation for the Exploitation of Meteorological Satellites (EUMETSAT) which operates the MetOp polar-orbiting satellites. NOAA is also responsible for cooperative activities with international partners who will assist with implementation of the NPOESS restructure. This coordination involves close contact with EUMETSAT, the Japan Aerospace Exploration Agency, the Centre National d'Études Spatiales, and the Department of National Defence-Canada. The Administration's decision to restructure NPOESS reaffirmed the importance of meeting the Nation's space-based environmental needs for sustained weather and climate observations from polar-orbiting satellites.

The Administration has also made substantial increases in funding as part of the FY2011 budget for NOAA's Satellite and Information Services portfolio and NASA's Earth Sciences program. NASA will be using this augmentation to address pressing scientific and national issues associated with climate change and the Nation's climate research and monitoring capabilities. As recommended by the NRC's Decadal Survey, this budget returns NASA Earth Science funding to the approximate level that it had in FY2000, an increase of more than 30% from recent levels. This funding allows for the acceleration and expansion of activities across the entire, coordinated Earth Science program—in the areas of flight missions, research, applications, and Earth Science mission technology development—thus advancing the balance and scope that have been hallmarks of NASA Earth System Science. In addition to building the Orbiting Carbon Observatory-2 mission for launch in 2013, NASA will: accelerate development of the four

NRC Decadal Survey Tier 1 missions so that they are all launched by 2017; accelerate and expand the Venture-class line of competed, innovative small missions; initiate new space missions to address continuity of high-priority climate observations; and bring two Decadal Survey Tier 2 missions forward to allow launch by 2020. Complementing the flight portfolio expansion, NASA will advance climate research, multiply applications using the full set of available (NASA and non-NASA) satellite measurements for direct societal benefit, and develop/mature technologies required for the next generation of Earth observing missions. The challenge that NOAA and NASA face is to develop the research to operations transition to ensure that the most promising NASA measurements are placed onto NOAA operational platforms.

The Administration also showed significant support for ocean observing by signing into law the Integrated Coastal and Ocean Observation System Act section of the Omnibus Public Land Management Act of 2009 (Public Law 111-11). In accordance with this Act, NOAA and other federal agencies engaged in ocean observing are continuing to build and sustain a system to provide critical ocean and coastal observations to regional, national and global end users. As part of the U.S. Global Change Research Program's (USGCRP) role in coordination of the federal climate change research portfolio across all the relevant agencies, the principal agency representatives to USGCRP reviewed NASA's draft plan for the FY2011 augmentation, and these reviews will be taken into account as NASA moves forward in implementing the plan. The Administration intends to utilize USGCRP in a similar manner in the future as a mechanism for ensuring broad federal coordination on climate observations.

The Administration will be drawing on the preliminary plan presented in this report to assist in the development of a comprehensive strategy for Earth observations. This report represents a first but significant step in developing a larger strategy for Earth observations.

Conclusions

Our ability to understand and respond to our changing planet hinges on timely scientific information and situational awareness. Information and understanding will continue to be the foundations of decision support in the face of uncertainty. Investments in Earth observations over the last 40 years have brought remarkable achievements in weather prediction, disaster prediction and response, land management, and our broad base of Earth science knowledge. Earth observation products provide, at a minimum, an additional $30 billion to the U.S. economy annually.[20]

The only way to know what is happening to our planet and to manage our resources wisely and proactively is to measure it. This means tracking changes decade after decade and reanalyzing the records in light of new insights, technologies, and methodologies. Our government has supported scientists in producing long-term Earth observation records, such as those for total column ozone and the amount of carbon dioxide in the atmosphere. Similarly, statistically-based surveys using oceanographic ships have documented some species, such as marine fish in the Northeast U.S., over time periods approaching five decades.[21] These high-quality, long-term data records and others like them have inevitably yielded dividends to our Nation vastly exceeding expectations. By enhancing development and deployment of observations, we can continue essential measurements and launch new observations that have the potential to improve our scientific ability in ways that could revolutionize our understanding of the planet.

U.S Government agencies are successfully working together to provide these observations to the public through well-known systems such as those of the National Weather Service, and also innovative collaborations such as the AIRNow air quality portal, the National Integrated Drought Information System (NIDIS), and international partnerships such as the Global Biodiversity Information Facility (GBIF). This infrastructure and support for data management, analysis, and use is frequently not costed out sufficiently when data collection systems are developed and built.

The crucial satellite and *in situ* observations currently made or outlined here will be of diminished utility unless we also sustain (1) effective data management of the observations collected; (2) large-scale numerical simulation capabilities in both government agencies and academia to explore scenarios using these observations; and (3) the scientists necessary to provide data stewardship expertise to ensure that the observations and products derived from them are made accessible to the various science and user communities that require them for both research and applications. These are all required to maintain and sustain U.S. leadership in Earth observations research; not least is the key need for leadership in basic science of adaptation to, and mitigation of, climate change. The satellite and *in situ* observations described in this report are complementary; and as such it is essential to bear in mind that satellite observations universally rely upon ground observations for calibration and validation, and that many current uses of satellite observations employ objective analyses to blend the high accuracy of *in situ* observation with the high spatial coverage provided from space-based platforms.

While this report highlights a number of areas for improving and integrating Earth observations, it does not consider the costs of implementing new Earth observation systems. Decisions to implement Earth observation systems should include consideration of costs, benefits, and availability of resources. This document provides a start; its principal offering is a set of priorities that is a pragmatic and incremental depiction of what is truly needed. Building on these priorities, the document also offers a preliminary plan, to be updated on an ongoing basis, for making progress toward these priorities. However, we see the emergence of a new paradigm that exploits the full value and possibilities of Earth observations in concert. So much can be achieved, but we must renew our national and international commitment to this life-sustaining infrastructure.

Table 2. USGEO Alphabetical Summary of Recommended Observations – Near-Term Gaps and Opportunities

These recommended observations are not meant to replace existing capabilities, but to build upon them in each of these key areas. They will be most useful when built on interoperable standards, widely distributed for use, and supported over time.

Measurement	Space-Based Recommendations and Status	*In situ* Recommendations and Status	Rationale	Linkages
Air Quality (gases and aerosols)	For space-based observations, the top operational and research need is more frequent and finer spatial resolution data. This could be done in coordination with any development and deployment of other geostationary or low-Earth orbit capabilities by international partners. NASA should proceed with the NRC Decadal Survey mission Geostationary Coastal and Air Pollution Events (GEOCAPE) after 2020.	NOAA should work towards implementing the recommendations of the 2004 NRC report, Air Quality Management in the United States. This report calls for enhancing the existent ground-based monitoring network by redistribution of current assets, prioritizing additional locations, deploying new technologies, and developing complementary capabilities to observe vertical profiles and utilize satellite observations. Have EPA sustain and advance current infrastructure such as the National Air Monitoring Stations/State and Local Air Monitoring Stations (NAMS/SLAMS), the National Core Multipollutant Monitoring Network, and the Photochemical Assessment Monitoring Stations (PAMS) with funds proposed in the 2011 Budget. Work towards implementing the recommendation contained in the 2008 NRC report, Observing Weather and Climate from the Ground Up: A Nationwide Network of Networks, to develop a surface-based mesoscale observing system to measure atmospheric pollutant composition. The recommendations include carbon monoxide, sulfur dioxide, ozone, and particulate matter less than 2.5 microns in size at approximately 200 urban and rural sites (~175 km spacing).	An improved ground-based monitoring network integrated with observations from geostationary Earth orbit, low Earth orbit, and suborbital platforms, as used by our national weather prediction system, is needed to derive a 4-dimensional view (3 spatial plus temporal) of air quality and the processes that drive it.	Health, Air Pollution, Climate, Wildfire

Measurement	Space-Based Recommendations and Status	*In situ* Recommendations and Status	Rationale	Linkages
Biodiversity	See Landscape Characterization/Vegetation	Support the Smithsonian Institution Global Earth Observatories (SIGEO), the National Ecological Observatory Network (NEON), the Long Term Ecological Research (LTER), and Experimental Forests and Ranges (EFR). Ensure the continuity of trending data collection programs like the Forest Service's Forest Inventory and Analysis (FIA) Program and the Natural Resources Conservation Service's National Resources Inventory (NRI). Continue to support NOAA's ocean and coastal living marine resoure and ecological/ecosystem surveys. The 2011 Budget provides funding to sustain the above programs.	*In situ* data are critical to measure ecosystem processes and disturbances such as invasive species, wildland fires, and altered phenology patterns. Existing programs such as the Global Biodiversity Information Facility, the Forest Inventory and Analysis (FIA) Program, and the National Resources Inventory (NRI) are vital in monitoring such ecosystem processes and effects, and assess their natural range of variations in relation to ongoing climate change and land management activities. Developing a National Phenology Network would strongly complement these activities. These networks are effective for this purpose but are currently too limited in scope to provide maximum management effectiveness and decision support. Marine ecosystems are managed under a number of Federal statutes including the Magnuson Stevens Fishery Conservation and management Act, the Marine Mammal Protection Act, the Endangered Species Act, the Coral Reef Conservation Act, the National Marine sanctuaries Act, and others. All of these statutes have observing requirements to assure adequate protections for the nation's marine resources.	Ecosystems, Pharmaceuticals, Climate, Agriculture, Health
Clouds/Aerosols	NASA is scheduled to launch Glory in 2010, a mission to measure black carbon soot and other aerosols. NASA currently has the option of proceeding with the NRC Decadal Survey Aerosol-Cloud-Ecosystems mission, a dedicated aerosol and cloud mission in combination with an ocean color instrument, after 2020. The 2011 Budget proposes an augmentation for development of an ocean color and clouds/aerosols polarimetry mission (launch in 2018) to bridge between existing on-orbit missions and the future, more capable ACE. NOAA and NASA should work toward producing a VIIRS JPSS imager capable of continuing MODIS' cloud climate data records.	Expand the Department of Energy's Atmospheric Radiation Measurement (ARM) Climate Research Facility (ACRF) ground networks and NASA's AErosol RObotic NETwork (AERONET) and Micro-Pulse Lidar Network (MPLNET). The 2011 Budget supports these efforts. NOAA should continue its measurement programs to reduce uncertainty in radiative forcing owing to both direct and indirect aerosol effects. These currently constitute the largest uncertainty in overall radiative forcing by gases and particles. This includes monitoring aerosol properties, distributions, and optical depth globally from ground and air-based systems, as well as targeted field missions. It also requires coordination of measurements internationally through WMO Global Atmospheric Watch (WMO/GAW), the Network for Detection of Atmospheric composition Change (NDACC), and the Global Climate Observing System (GCOS).	There is a potential degradation in global aerosol satellite measurements due to the inferior performance of the VIIRS instrument's aerosol channels and no near-term replacement for the Multi-angle Imaging Spectro-Radiometer (MISR) instrument on NASA's Terra satellite. *In situ* aerosol measurements from the AERONET autonomous network, and cloud, aerosol, precipitation, and radiation observations from the ACRF network are key in addressing high-priority climate change questions.	Weather Forecasting, Earth Radiation Budget, Climate, Water Availability, Solar Energy Resources

Measurement	Space-Based Recommendations and Status	*In situ* Recommendations and Status	Rationale	Linkages
Coastal Zone	Continue to support existing systems.	Support the Integrated Ocean Observing System (IOOS) to maintain observations and networks to support coastal climate mitigation and adaptation, human health threats, and ecosystem management. Key components include buoy and coastal station networks, high frequency coastal radars, the development of *in situ* sensors for rapid detection of pathogens, harmful algae, and toxins, and exploitation of new cost-effective technologies such as ocean gliders. Improve the capability for assessing hypoxia and its impacts by prioritizing the number of observation systems (platforms and gliders) measuring dissolved oxygen in coastal waters. The 2011 budget supports these efforts.	With coastal development continuing at a rapid pace, society is becoming increasingly vulnerable to water quality issues, and sea level rise. While the oceans provide resources critical to human survival and well-being, they also pose dangers. At present there are major gaps in our capability to provide timely and accurate measurements of waterborne pathogens, toxic algae, and other toxins. Automated monitoring of coastal environments can provide real-time or near-real-time data at spatial and temporal scales not possible with current monitoring networks. There are also near-shore measurement gaps in winds, temperature, salinity, waves, and currents on time and space scales relevant to the dynamics of waterborne pathogens and harmful algae, as well as to navigation and safety of port operations. Finally, there are gaps in our ability to measure nutrient sources, combined sewer outfalls, and other point and non-point contamination sources along the coasts.	Coastal Ocean Health, Human Health, Climate, Disasters
Earth Radiation Budget/ Total Solar Irradiance	NASA should continue plans to launch Glory in 2010, a mission to observe aerosols and total solar irradiance, the latter with a continuation of the SORCE TIM instrument. NOAA and NASA should continue development and remanifestation of Clouds and the Earth's Radiant Energy System (CERES) for Earth radiation budget data on NPP and JPSS, and launch the remanifested Total Solar Irradiance Sensor (TSIS) as soon as a launch vehicle has been identified by the JPSS program. CERES is now scheduled to fly on the first JPSS satellite; options for carrying TSIS on orbit are under review.	Maintain and expand the AErosol RObotic NETwork (AERONET) and the Department of Energy's Atmospheric Radiation Measurement (ARM) Climate Research Facility (ACRF) ground networks. NOAA and DOE should continue their support of the Baseline Surface Radiation Network, the Surface Energy Budget Network, and other surface radiation measurements to provide independent information on trends, distributions, and fluxes of radiant energy, and to aid in validating satellite retrievals. International activities should be continued to ensure global coverage and consistency of measurements. The 2011 Budget supports these efforts.	Solar radiant energy is the major driver of the Earth's climate. The input of energy from the sun is understood increasingly well since total solar irradiance measurements from space began in 1978. This measurement must be continued, as it is the main driver of climate and the only source of climate variability that we have been able to measure. The amount of radiation leaving the Earth through the complex system of clouds, aerosols, atmospheric constituents, oceans, ice, and land surfaces provides a quantitative, system level check of global climate model results. Accurate measurements of the Earth's radiation budget have also been made since 1978 from satellite instruments designed for this purpose. There are currently potential gaps in the continuity of these measurements.	Climate, Weather Forecasting, Solar Renewable Energy

Measurement	Space-Based Recommendations and Status	*In situ* Recommendations and Status	Rationale	Linkages
Fires	Ensure the VIIRS instrument is sufficient for maintaining the fire climate data record. A spatial resolution to 100 meters for visible/infrared bands, and 500 meters for the thermal bands, with coverage every 6 hours is highly desirable. Develop LDCM data at a 30 meter spatial resolution.	Support the continued development and deployment of *in situ* fire monitoring capabilities and sensors for manned and unmanned aerial platforms supporting tactical fire management and fire research at USDA, NIST, and NOAA.	There is a potential degradation in capability in satellite-based fire detection and monitoring. Manned aircraft are an important data source for tactical fire information such as active fire perimeters, hotspots, and fire spread; information that is critical for incident management. Unmanned aircraft are a useful capability.	Disasters, Wildfires, Public Safety, Forestry, Ecosystems
GeoHazard and Deformation Monitoring	NASA should launch the radar portion of the NRC Decadal Survey mission Deformation, Ecosystem Structure, and Dynamics of Ice (DESDynI) mission. If necessary, the lidar and radar instruments on DESDynI can be flown on different platforms. The L-Band Interferometric Synthetic Aperture Radar (InSAR) will provide surface deformation measurements. The 2011 Budget provides an augmentation over previous budget plans for NASA to launch DESDynI mission in 2017.	For surface deformation, sustain the geodetic monitoring capabilities of Earthscope. For earthquakes and tsunami, implement the Advanced National Seismic System (ANSS), and sustain the capabilities of the Global Seismographic Network (GSN). Expand the number of offshore seismic nodes in the Ocean Observatories Initiative (OOI). For volcanic activity, USGS is implementing the National Volcano Early Warning System (NVEWS). For the geodetic reference frame, sustain the U.S. supported capabilities of the Global Navigation Satellite System (GNSS) network. The 2011 Budget provides funding to support these efforts. It also provides an increase to USGS to invest in the Advanced National Seismic System and National Volcano Early Warning System.	Represents a major gap. High-resolution digital topography is a key unmet need for many disasters, including earthquakes, volcanic eruptions and landslides. Currently there is no global capability to monitor changes to topography (deformation). The seismic and volcano monitoring networks suffer gaps and inadequate refresh of aging infrastructure. A program for improved monitoring of volcanoes, the National Volcano Early Warning System, has been developed.	Disasters, Earthquakes, Volcanoes, Landslides, Polar Ice Sheets
Gravity	NASA should sustain observations of the time-varying gravity field from the Gravity Recovery and Climate Experiment (GRACE-1) and launch GRACE-FO in 2016 ("FO" for "Follow ON"), a gap-filler mission with the same capabilities and characteristics as GRACE-1. The 2011 Budget provides funding for GRACE FO to be launched in 2016. NASA should plan for a follow-on GRACE-2 mission in 2020 to continue estimating changes in ocean mass, terrestrial water storage, and ice sheet mass.	NOAA's Gravity for the Redefinition of the American Vertical Datum (GRAV-D) program has the goal of collecting gravity data for a new national vertical datum by 2023 which will allow improvement in elevations through GPS technology to an accuracy of ~2cm compared to 2m today, with profound implications for all activities relying on accurate heights. Sustain NOAA's Deep-ocean Assessment and Reporting of Tsunamis (DART) network of ocean bottom pressure recorders. These data are crucial for calibrating GRACE gravity field measurements. The 2011 Budget provides funding for NOAA to continue the GRAV-D FY10 initiative and to improve the DART network.	Gravity measurements provide breakthrough capability in estimating changes in ocean mass, terrestrial water storage, and ice sheet mass. Continuity of gravity observations is crucial for climate understanding.	Climate, Water Availability, Oceans, Polar Ice Sheets

Measurement	Space-Based Recommendations and Status	*In situ* Recommendations and Status	Rationale	Linkages
Greenhouse Gases	NASA should launch a replacement for the Orbiting Carbon Observatory (OCO), lost in February 2009, in 2013 and build a spare OCO instrument for possible launch in 2015-2017. The outcome of the OCO mission should be used to evaluate the technical approach for the next generation greenhouse gas sensors. The 2011 Budget proposes to launch the OCO-2 in 2013 and proposes $171 million in FY 2011 for the mission. NASA should plan to evaluate different laser sounder instruments for measuring atmospheric CO_2 as called for in the ASCENDS Decadal Survey mission. The laser CO_2 sounder instruments could complement OCO and provide a great density of measurements through their day and night duty cycle. NASA may consider additional testing that could include aircraft or other platforms to mitigate risk. NASA should also undertake research to monitor CH_4 from space.	Support NOAA's ground and air-based measurements of greenhouse gases to provide accurate, independent measures of the trends, distributions and fluxes of CO_2 and other greenhouse gases (e.g., N_2O, CH_4, halocarbons), to aid in verifying satellite retrievals, and to provide needed information on trace gases for refining transport models and emission sources. Support NOAA's measurements of carbon and dissolved oxygen from ocean carbon survey vessels and on a subset of the Argo float array to further understand carbon sequestration and carbon cycle-climate feedbacks and ocean acidification. Support ship-based efforts to systematically collect full water column data on ocean carbon, such as the U.S. Global Ocean Carbon and Repeat Hydrography Program. Support the interagency AmeriFlux network that provides continuous observations of ecosystem level exchanges of CO_2, water, energy and momentum spanning diurnal, synoptic, seasonal, and interannual time scales and is currently composed of sites from North America, Central America, and South America. NOAA and NASA should continue their support of international coordinating mechanisms through WMO (particularly Global Atmospheric Watch), Global Climate Observing System and its supporting panels, and the intergovernmental Group on Earth Observations (GEO) to ensure that global observing systems are coordinated and comparable and to maximize benefit of international observing systems.	Greenhouse gases are key elements of the global climate system. The 50-year record of atmospheric carbon dioxide made by NOAA's global cooperative air sampling network serves as the observational foundation of our understanding of how greenhouse gas concentrations are increasing. Atmospheric, terrestrial, and oceanic observations are essential for determining the functional relationships between carbon fluxes, disturbance, and environmental variables is essential to improving understanding of the carbon cycle. It is known that the ocean stores at least 50 times more carbon than the atmosphere. Understanding the global carbon cycle depends on monitoring carbon cycling within the ocean and the air-sea exchange of carbon dioxide. Carbon up-take by the ocean is altering the acidity of seawater, which is threatening marine animals. Terrestrial ecosystems contain 4 times the carbon residing in the global atmosphere. Terrestrial carbon stocks located on or near the earth's surface are subject to rapidly changing global environmental conditions. A focus of terrestrial carbon cycle research remains the determination of the fate and rate of net carbon release from ecosystems under projected rapid rates of climate change.	Climate, Health, Ecosystems

Measurement	Space-Based Recommendations and Status	In situ Recommendations and Status	Rationale	Linkages
Landscape Characterization/ Vegetation	Continue improvements to the Visible/ Infrared Imagery Radiometer Suite (VIIRS) instrument scheduled to be deployed on NPP and JPSS. Evaluate an operational moderate-resolution satellite program that would meet the land imaging needs of U.S. civil agencies and society, in accordance with the OSTP-led Future of Land Imaging Interagency Working Group's recommendations in the 2007 document "A Plan for a U.S. National Land Imaging Program." Planning for Landsat-9 is being undertaken by the USGS and NASA, in cooperation with other stake-holders. This planning, however, must look beyond Landsat 9 and lay out requirements for an operational Landsat program. Recommendations for future Landsat-like instruments include a spatial resolution of at most 20 meters, at least a 5-day repeat cycle, increased daily acquisition rates, and possibly additional visual shortwave infrared and thermal infrared spectral bands. Additional higher spatial-resolution imagery will still be required to understand field-level conditions. These data could be acquired from commercial sources, or by the Federal government if the commercial sources do not meet requirements. NASA and USGS are moving forward toward an LDCM launch in 2012. NASA plans to launch the Deformation, Ecosystem Structure, and Dynamics of Ice (DESDynI) mission in 2017 to provide canopy height and structure measurements. DESDynI is an important carbon cycle climate mission for providing forest biomass and carbon globally. As such, it will be key to identifying the forest carbon sink of ~30% of current global CO_2 emissions. In addition, it will provide laser altimetry and SAR data from ice sheets. If necessary, the DESDynI lidar and DESDynI radar could be separated and flown on different platforms. The 2011 Budget requests a $679 million increase for the JPSS program that includes continued development of VIIRS toward a target delivery date of FY 2013. It also requests a $13.35 million increase to the USGS to accommodate ground system requirements changes for LDCM.	Sustain the National Agriculture Imagery Program (NAIP) and the follow-on program Imagery for the Nation (IFTN). The 2011 Budget continues NAIP.	There is an imminent gap in the Landsat series of satellites. Landsat has provided land images used for global land cover mapping, estimating agricultural production, and estimating forest diversity. The utility and importance of moderate-resolution land imaging data have been well proven but the Nation has no permanent, operational Landsat-like land-imaging program. The current Landsat 5 and 7 missions are already past their nominal design life, and the next Landsat in the series, the Landsat Data Continuity Mission (LDCM), is not expected to launch until late 2012. The looming gap in this 38-year record will impact not only agriculture and forestry, but also our understanding of the carbon cycle, and ecosystem monitoring. Science missions, which by their nature do not provide sustained data over time, are not a reliable source of the earth observations that are critical to land-use and change research. Operational limitations coupled with the near certainty of a Landsat data gap have forced key traditional Landsat users like USDA to go outside the US to attempt to satisfy moderate-resolution requirements. Increased spatial and temporal resolution are critical to support sustainable agriculture. Scientists have been able to exploit data from sensors that were not intended for observations of the landscape, such as the Advanced Very High Resolution Radiometer (AVHRR) with its 29-year record, and cross calibrate them with Landsat with its 38-year record and the Moderate Resolution Imaging Spectroradiometer (MODIS) with its 10-year record. The AVHRR-MODIS time series will be continued by the VIIRS instruments on the NPP and JPSS.	Ecosystems, Climate, Agriculture, Disaster Response, Wildfire Assessment

Measurement	Space-Based Recommendations and Status	*In situ* Recommendations and Status	Rationale	Linkages
Ocean Color	NOAA and NASA continue to pursue international partnerships (e.g., the European Space Agency (ESA), the Japanese Space Agency (JAXA), and the Indian Space Research Organization (ISRO)) to provide risk mitigation strategies for ocean color measurements. Should VIIRS not meet ocean color requirements, investigate improvements to VIIRS to meet this requirement. The 2011 Budget provides an augmentation over previous budget plans for NASA to begin development of the Pre-Aerosol, Clouds, and Ocean Ecosystem (PACE) mission for launch in 2018. For the long term, proceed with the ocean color component of NASA's ACE Decadal Survey mission as a potential complement to VIIRS. The option of a stand-alone mission that is a copy of SeaWiFS, or an international exchange of instruments on a joint space mission should only be pursued if VIIRS will not meet the requirement. When released, the results of the National Research Council Committee on Assessing Requirements for Sustained Ocean Color Research and Operations study should be used to refine the satellite strategy. The FY 2011 Budget includes a $679 million increase for the JPSS program.	Sustain the NASA-NOAA Marine Optical Buoy (MOBY) program and the AERONET-Maritime Aerosol Network. Ocean color *in situ* validation efforts and the intercomparison of ocean color measurements among satellite ocean color instruments depend on these observations, and the FY 2011 Budget supports these programs.	Today's satellite ocean color radiometry data form the backbone of assessing primary productivity and carbon cycling in the ocean, supporting fisheries and integrated ecosystem assessments, and measuring and monitoring coastal and ocean habitat changes, and climate impacts. However, this continuous and consistent climate-quality record is presently at risk of being interrupted. The SeaWiFS mission launched in 1997 has experienced "outages" during which data are not available. Similarly, the MODIS instrument on Aqua was launched in 2002 and, though currently in good health, is also past its expected lifetime. The follow-on ocean color instruments are the VIIRS instruments on NPP and JPSS. It is presently unclear if the first VIIRS sensor will have the same capability as SeaWiFS, however, subsequent VIIRS units may reestablish the data record and this is the desired source of ocean color climate data records.	Climate, Health, Oceans
Ocean Surface Vector Winds (OSVW)	NOAA and NASA should establish a sustained source for OSVW information to maintain and improve upon the significant gains in operational marine wind forecasting and warning capability realized from the QuikSCAT OSVW data. International partnerships may also provide cost-effective opportunities to sustain this capability.	Maintain the airborne Stepped Frequency Microwave Radiometer (SFMR) capability aboard the Hurricane Hunter WC-130J and NOAA's P-3 aircraft, and support follow-on technologies such as the Hurricane Intensity Radiometer (HIRAD) which shows promise to provide improved prediction of hurricane intensity and will provide measurements through precipitation. Maintain the existing array of fixed and drifting surface data buoys.	The value and capability of satellite-based ocean surface vector winds (OSVW) measurements was clearly demonstrated with over nine years of nearly continuous OSVW data from the NASA's polar orbiting QuikSCAT satellite. These measurements proved to be of important value for climate studies and revolutionized operational marine weather warnings, analyses, and forecasting within National Weather Service (NWS) offices. QuikSCAT provided critical wind data that enabled NWS to significantly improve the accuracy of hurricane force wind warnings in the offshore regions of the Atlantic and Pacific oceans for non-tropical ocean storms, and for tropical storms in the Pacific Ocean.	Climate, Weather Forecasting, Transportation, Ocean, Hurricanes

Measurement	Space-Based Recommendations and Status	*In situ* Recommendations and Status	Rationale	Linkages
Precipitation	NASA should launch the joint U.S. and Japan Global Precipitation Measurement (GPM) mission to reduce the likely gap in the rainfall measurement record provided by the Tropical Rainfall Measurement Mission (TRMM). The 2011 Budget provides an augmentation over previous budget plans for NASA to launch the GPM mission in 2013.	Sustain NOAA's U.S. Climate Reference Network (USCRN) and continue work on NOAA's Surface Energy Budget Network (SEBN) and the Historical Climatology Network-Modernization (HCN-M) to provide ground-based precipitation measurements. Maintain the Nation's NEXRAD network and move toward a dual polarization capability for NEXRAD. Dual polarization will provide the capability to discriminate between precipitation types and provide a significant improvement in estimating rainfall rates. Support the Department of Energy's Atmospheric Radiation Measurement (ARM) Climate Research Facility (ACRF) ground networks. ACRF's addition of new scanning precipitation radars as well as scanning dual frequency cloud radars provides a strong capability for characterizing cloud properties and linking with precipitation processes. The 2011 Budget supports the new DOE capabilities and proposes additional NEXRAD funding for acquisition and deployment of Dual polarization technology.	Precipitation is the centerpiece of our planet's hydrological cycle, and understanding it is crucial to unraveling many of the uncertainties about climate change and its impacts. Precipitation measurements are also critical for flood and landslide prediction, agricultural productivity, spread of disease, ecosystem health, water availability, and energy production. There is currently a looming gap of satellite measurement beyond the Tropical Rainfall Measurement Mission (TRMM).	Weather Forecasting, Flooding, Landslides, Climate, Agriculture, Disease Vectors, Water Availability, Ecosystem Health, Hydroelectric and Biomass Renewable Energy Production, Disasters

Measurement	Space-Based Recommendations and Status	*In situ* Recommendations and Status	Rationale	Linkages
Sea Level	The sea level rise problem requires a comprehensive observing system approach, built around the measurement of sea level and the contributions to sea level change from both mass and density changes. NOAA and EUMETSAT should continue their Jason partnership by extending the current generation of altimeters with Jason-3, scheduled for launch in 2013, and Jason-CS, a series of advanced follow-on missions beginning in 2018. NOAA should also continue, working in collaboration with other space agencies through the CEOS Ocean Surface Topography Virtual Constellation to ensure maximum benefit from the set of international sea level altimeter missions. To determine the mass contributions from the melting of grounded ice and other continental sources, NASA should continue the GRACE gravity measurements (see Gravity Section), launch Ice, Cloud, and land Elevation Satellite-2 (ICESat-2) in 2015, proceed with the Landsat Data Continuity Mission (LDCM) and DESDynI radar mission to measure outlet glacier velocities, and proceed with the DESDynI lidar mission to continue beyond ICESat-2 crucial altimetry of ice sheets. The FY 2011 Budget fully funds Jason-3.	In conjunction with the Jason program, it is important to maintain the 220+ sea-level tide gauges, the U.S. portion of the integrated Global Ocean Observing System (GOOS), and incorporate Global Positioning System (GPS) capability. Tide gauge observations are essential for calibrating altimeter observations and, in some cases, provide a long (100 year) record useful for interpreting current trends. And, to monitor and understand the density contributions to sea level change, it is important that NOAA continue supporting the Argo float array to monitor heat in the upper ocean, add a capability to provide deep ocean (>2000 down to 5000 m) profile measurements, and deploy real-time-reporting ocean-bottom-mounted arrays to monitor changing ocean circulation and global heat transport.	Rising sea level is critical to coastal population safety and welfare, to predicting storm surge and coastal inundation from tropical storms, and for maritime safety of navigation. *In situ* measurements are needed to understand the underlying cause and rate of sea level rise.	Climate Change, Coastal Development and Safety, Disasters, Commerce and Marine Transportation
Soil Moisture	The European Space Agency has recently launched and is successfully operating the Soil Moisture and Ocean Salinity (SMOS) mission. Proceed with the NASA Soil Moisture Active-Passive (SMAP) mission to augment this urgently needed data record. The 2011 Budget provides an augmentation over previous budget plans for NASA to launch the SMAP mission in 2014.	Sustain NOAA's U.S. Climate Reference Network (USCRN) and USDA's Soil Climate Analysis Network (SCAN) *in situ* soil moisture networks. Work to implement the 2008 National Research Council recommendation of a national, real-time network of soil moisture observations at approximately 3000 sites.	There is a strong potential to significantly advance in long-range weather and seasonal forecasting. Global soil moisture measurements can provide improved early warning and decision support for droughts, better predictions of agricultural productivity, and improved flood forecasts. Key indicator for heat stress, waterborne infectious diseases, disease vectors, and zoonotic diseases.	Agriculture, Drought, Flooding, Weather and Climate Forecasting, Water Cycle Processes, Disease Vectors, Health, Biomass Renewable Energy
Solar Wind and Magnetic Storms	Refurbish the Deep Space Climate Observatory (DSCOVR) satellite and its solar wind sensors to replace the Advanced Composition Explorer (ACE) capability. The 2011 Budget provides NOAA $9.5 million for the DSCOVR mission.	USGS should modernize the ground-based geomagnetic observatories.	It is important to maintain the continuity of advanced warning of geomagnetic storms impacting power grids, satellite operations and communications.	Energy, Disaster, Communications, Satellite Operations

Measurement	Space-Based Recommendations and Status	*In situ* Recommendations and Status	Rationale	Linkages
Water Quantity and Quality	NASA should continue its observations of gravity fields from GRACE-1 and follow-on gravity missions for ground water storage and ice sheet mass variations. In addition, NOAA and NASA seek international partnerships to complement JPSS's ability to understand ground water and snow water equivalent (e.g., the AMSR-2/3 instruments on JAXA's GCOM mission).	Support the modernization of the Nation's 7,000 stream gauges by replacing obsolete telemetry to ensure continued real-time operations and provide more timely information needed for better water management. Consider supplying more opportunities to study large river basins. Investigate and implement new technologies to measure sediment in rivers. Also support the Advisory Committee on Water Information, and the National Water Quality Monitoring Council plan for sustaining and enhancing the Nation's capability to monitor water quality. Continue to improve snow moisture measurements such as SNOwpack TELemetry (SNOTEL) and the NOAA Operational Hydrology Program to increase understanding of source water from snow and runoff. The FY 2011 Budget supports these efforts through the WaterSMART initiative, which invests an additional $9 million for a multi-year, nationwide study of water availability and use.	Full understanding of the quantity and quality of our waters, and particularly our ability to locate problems and provide timely and accurate warning to the public depends on a robust monitorning system.	Water Availability, Water Quality, Flood, Streamflow, Water Resources Forecasting, Health, Agriculture, Hydroelectric and Biomass Renewable Energy Production, Sustainable Growth

SUPPLEMENT

This supplement provides more detailed information and selected references for the recommended priorities listed in Table 2. The supplement also provides a preliminary implementation plan for achieving these options, and recent Administration actions and the proposed 2011 Budget begin to address these priorities. These recommendations build on a methodology applied by USGEO that naturally arose from the structure of the Strategic Plan for the U.S. Integrated Earth Observation System (IEOS), which defines the concept of Societal Benefit Areas (SBAs). This assessment focused on measurements having multiple benefits across SBAs and measurements deemed critical to an individual SBA. Within that subset, measurements that were assessed as being particularly at risk or holding great promise for providing dramatic gains or a scientific breakthrough were identified. In completing this assessment, the SAG assumed that some systems funded and currently under development, such as the NPOESS Preparatory Project (NPP), JPSS and GOES-R, will be successfully put into operation.

Air Quality (Gases and Aerosols):

Air quality affects human health, other living organisms, and climate. While much has been done in the last forty years to improve air quality, it is still a cause of illness in many parts of the Nation, and cleaning up our air can provide an effective near-term opportunity for climate change mitigation. Typically, air is monitored for several pollutants including particulate matter, nitrogen compounds, sulfur compounds, carbon monoxide, volatile organic hydrocarbons, and ozone. Over the next several decades, the existing ground-based monitoring system, which consists of about 6,000 monitoring sites across the country, and operated at a cost of about $200M per year, will be inadequate to meet the challenges of air quality management and prediction. Furthermore, maintaining funding for this system is challenging, even though the current investment in air quality monitoring is a fraction of a percent of the annual costs of complying with the Clean Air Act or the economic benefits associated with clean air.

An improved ground-based monitoring network integrated with observations from geostationary Earth orbit, low Earth orbit, and suborbital platforms, as used by our national weather prediction system, would be needed to derive a 4-dimensional view (3 spatial plus temporal) of air quality and the processes that drive it. The 2008 National Research Council publication, *Observing Weather and Climate from the Ground Up: A Nationwide Network of Networks*, recommends the development of mesoscale observational capabilities to enable air quality prediction. Surface-based observations of carbon monoxide, sulfur dioxide, ozone, and particulate matter less than 2.5 microns in size are important because they may impact human health, they serve as precursors to additional hazardous compounds, and they can help to extend the utility of parameters observed from space.

Recommendations:

For space-based observations, the top operational and research need is more frequent and finer spatial resolution data. The NRC Decadal Survey mission Geostationary Coastal and Air Pollution Events (GEOCAPE) would provide this capability, and NASA should explore proceeding with GEOCAPE after 2020. This could be done in coordination with any development and deployment of other geostationary, low-Earth orbit, and ground-based capabilities by international partners. The implementation of the recommendations of the 2004 NRC report, *Air Quality Management in the United States* would provide complementary *in situ* observations. NASA should review the existent ground-based monitoring network with respect to the redistribution of current assets, addition of additional locations, deployment of new technologies, and development of complementary capabilities to observe vertical profiles and utilize satellite observations. EPA should sustain its National Air Monitoring Stations/State and Local Air Monitoring Stations (NAMS/SLAMS), the National Core Multi-pollutant Monitoring Network, and the Photochemical Assessment Monitoring Stations (PAMS). NOAA should work towards implementing the recommendation contained in the 2008 NRC report, *Observing Weather and Climate from the Ground Up: A Nationwide Network of Networks*, to develop a surface-based mesoscale observing system to measure atmospheric pollutant composition. This should include carbon monoxide, sulfur dioxide, ozone, and particulate matter less than 2.5 microns in size at approximately 200 urban and rural sites (~175 km spacing).

Status:

The 2011 Budget partially supports these efforts.

Selected Reference(s):

National Research Council, *Earth Science and Applications from Space: National Imperatives for the Next Decade and Beyond*, National Academies Press, Washington DC, 2007

National Research Council, *Air Quality Management in the United States*, National Academies Press, Washington DC, 2004

National Research Council, *Observing Weather and Climate from the Ground Up: A Nationwide Network of Networks*, Committee on Developing Mesoscale Meteorological Observational Capabilities to Meet Multiple Needs, National Academies Press, Washington DC, 2008

http://aeronet.gsfc.nasa.gov/

http://www.epa.gov/cludygxb/programs/namslam.html

Biodiversity:

In general, ecology and biodiversity observation data use weather, climate, water, disaster, health, agriculture, and energy observation systems to effectively model the patterns and structures of ecosystems and their responses to changes in climate and human activities. Additional information on species occurrences, species interactions, life histories and ecological structure must be added to the geo-climatic models in order to understand the local patterns affecting organisms and communities. Ground-based networks, such as the Smithsonian Institution Global Earth Observatories (SIGEO), National Ecological Observatory Network (NEON), Long Term Ecological Research (LTER), Experimental Forests and Ranges (EFR), and the Census of Marine Life are critical to understanding and monitoring biodiversity and other ecosystem attributes in the needed spatial and temporal domains. *In situ* data are also necessary to measure ecosystem processes and disturbances such as invasive species, wildland fires, and altered phenology patterns. Existing programs such as the Global Biodiversity Information Facility (GBIF), the Forest Inventory and Analysis (FIA) Program, and the National Resources Inventory (NRI) are vital in monitoring such ecosystem processes and effects, and assess their natural range of variations in relation to ongoing climate change and land management activities. Developing a National Phenology Network would strongly complement these activities. These networks are effective for this purpose but are currently too limited in scope to provide maximum management effectiveness and decision support. The time series of ocean ecological surveys conducted by NOAA in support of its statutory missions represents the most complete set of ocean and coastal biodiversity measurements supported by the Federal government.

Recommendations:

Support the Smithsonian Institution Global Earth Observatories (SIGEO), National Ecological Observatory Network (NEON), the Long Term Ecological Research (LTER), and Experimental Forests and Ranges (EFR) networks.

Ensure the continuity of trending data collection programs like the Forest Service's Forest Inventory and Analysis (FIA) Program and the Natural Resources Conservation Service's National Resources Inventory (NRI). Continue to support NOAA's ocean and coastal living marine resource and ecological/ecosystem surveys.

Status:

The 2011 Budget continues to support and expand SIGEO and initiate construction of NEON. It also sustains funding for LTER, and EFR. The 2011 Budget provides funding to support FIA and NRI.

Selected Reference(s):

The H. John Heinz III Center for Science, Economics and the Environment, *Filling the Gaps: Priority Data Needs and Key Management Challenges for National Reporting on Ecosystem Condition*, May 2006, http://www.heinzctr.org/Programs/Reporting/ Working%20Groups/Data%20Gaps/Gaps_LongReport_LoRes.pdf

Environmental Information: Status of Federal Data Programs That Support Ecological Indicators, 2005, GAO 05-376, http://www.gao.gov/new.items/d05376.pdf

United States Department of Agriculture Forest Service, FS-865, *Forest Inventory and Analysis Strategic Plan*, January 2007

NSTC Joint Subcommittee on Ocean Science and Technology, *Charting the Course for Ocean Science in the Next Decade: An Ocean Research Priorities Plan and Implementation Strategy*," January 2007 http://ocean.ceq.gov/about/docs/orppfinal.pdf

United States Department of Commerce, *National Marine Fisheries Service 2001, Marine Fisheries Stock Assessment Improvement Plan*, National Oceanic and Atmospheric Administration, U.S. Department of Commerce, October 2001. http://www.st.nmfs.noaa.gov/StockAssessment/tm_spo56/saipafrontmatter.pdf

United States Department of Commerce, National Marine Fisheries Service, *A Requirements Plan for Improving the Understanding Of the Status of U.S. Protected Marine Species. Report of the NOAA Fisheries National Task Force for Improving Marine Mammal and Turtle Stock Assessments*. U.S. Department of Commerce, 2004, NOAA Tech. Memo. NMFS-F/SPO-63, 112 p

Clouds and Aerosols:

The climate science community is facing an interruption of key global aerosol satellite measurements due to the potential for inferior performance of the Visible/Infrared Imagery Radiometer Suite (VIIRS) instrument's aerosol channels and the fact that there is no near-term replacement for the Multi-angle Imaging SpectroRadiometer (MISR) instrument on NASA's Terra satellite. The combination of Moderate Resolution Imaging Spectroradiometer (MODIS) and Multi-angle Imaging SpectroRadiometer (MISR) satellite data has proven to be extremely useful for producing global aerosol measurements. These data, coupled with data from NASA's "A-Train" sensors, have advanced aerosol remote sensing and given aerosol studies a maturity heretofore absent. The contributions of *in situ* aerosol information from the AErosol RObotic NETwork (AERONET) autonomous network have greatly advanced our understanding of aerosol effects upon climate. The Department of Energy's Atmospheric Radiation Measurement (ARM) Climate Research Facility (ACRF) observations provide the long-term record of clouds, aerosols, and radiation needed to address high priority climate change science questions. Recently added instrumentation at the ACRF sites will provide data to span the aerosol-cloud-precipitation spectrum.

Recommendations:

Work towards producing a JPSS VIIRS imager that is capable of continuing MODIS' cloud climate data records. Expand the Department of Energy's Atmospheric Radiation Measurement (ARM) Climate Research Facility (ACRF) ground networks and NASA's AErosol RObotic NETwork (AERONET) and Micro-Pulse Lidar Network (MPLNET).

NOAA should continue its measurement programs to reduce uncertainty in radiative forcing owing to both direct and indirect aerosol effects. These currently constitute the largest uncertainty in overall radiative forcing by gases and particles. This includes monitoring aerosol properties, distributions, and optical depth globally from ground and air-based systems, as well as targeted field missions. It also requires coordination of measurements internationally through WMO Global Atmospheric Watch (WMO/GAW), the Network for Detection of Atmospheric composition Change (NDACC), and the Global Climate Observing System (GCOS).

Status:

NASA is scheduled to launch Glory in 2010, a mission to measure black carbon soot and other aerosols. The 2011 Budget proposes an augmentation for development of an ocean color and clouds/aerosols polarimetry mission (launch in 2018) to bridge between existing on-orbit missions and the future, more capable Aerosol-Cloud-Ecosystem (ACE) mission. The 2011 Budget sustains funding for the AERONET, MPLNET, and ACRF programs.

Selected Reference(s):

Yu, H., Y.J. Kaufman, M. Chin, G. Feingold, L.A. Remer, T.L. Anderson, Y. Balkanski, N. Bellouin, O. Boucher, S. Christopher, P. L. DeCola, R. Kahn, D. Koch, N. Loeb, M. S. Reddy, M. Schulz, T. Takemura, M. Zhou, "A review of measurement-based assessment of the aerosol direct radiative effect and forcing," Atmos. Chem. Phys., 6, 613–666, 2006, www.atmos-chem-phys.net/6/613/2006/

National Research Council, *Earth Science and Applications from Space: National Imperatives for the Next Decade and Beyond*, National Academies Press, Washington DC, 2007

DOE/SC-ARM-0803, *Contributions of the Atmospheric Radiation measurement (ARM) Program and the ARM Climate Research Facility to the U.S. Climate Change Science Program*, September 2008

DOE/SC-ARM-0804, ARM Climate Research Facility Workshop Report, November 2008, http://www.arm.gov/publications/programdocs/doe-sc-arm-0804.pdf

CCSP, 2008, *Synthesis and Assessment Product 5.1: Uses and Limitations of Observations, Data, Forecasts, and Other Projections in Decision Support for Selected Sectors and Regions*, Washington DC

Information about AERONET at: http://aeronet.gsfc.nasa.gov/

Coastal Zone:

The coastal zone changed profoundly during the 20th century, primarily due to growing populations and increasing urbanization. With coastal development continuing at a rapid pace, society is becoming increasingly vulnerable to water quality issues, and sea level rise. Rising sea levels will contribute to increased storm surges and flooding, even if hurricane intensities do not increase in response to the warming of the oceans. Climate change will impact coastal communities and living marine resources through factors including sea level rise, loss of Arctic sea ice, changes in fresh water regimes, ocean acidification, and patterns of resource abundance and phenology. U.S. Government plans for increasing observations of these phenomena are necessary to respond to these increasing threats.

While the oceans provide resources critical to human survival and well-being, aquatic toxins and pathogens can be damaging. Although probably significantly underestimated, the overall economic effects of harmful algal blooms alone in the U.S. (not including freshwater outbreaks) are at least $82 million per year, with public health costs of illness accounting for 45% of the total.

Automated monitoring of coastal environments can facilitate the examination of broad-scale patterns of pathogenic organism distributions, and provide real-time or near-real-time data at spatial and temporal scales not possible with current monitoring networks. We recommend prioritizing the development of biological sensors to detect pathogens, harmful algae, toxins and other contaminants and water quality to provide essential data for public health. The Advisory Committee on Water Information and the National Water Quality Monitoring Council's plan, the "National Water Quality Monitoring Network for U.S. Coastal Waters and Their Tributaries" was prepared at the behest of the National Science and Technology Council (NSTC) and the Council on Environmental Quality (CEQ). This document relates stress in freshwater tributaries to these coastal waters and to the mission of the Integrated Ocean Observing System (IOOS) monitoring network.

Recommendations:

Sustain investment in the Integrated Ocean Observing System (IOOS) to maintain observations and networks to support coastal climate mitigation and adaptation, human health threats, and ecosystem management. Key components include buoy and coastal station networks, high frequency coastal radars, the development of *in situ* sensors for rapid detection of pathogens, harmful algae, and toxins, and exploitation of new cost-effective technologies such as ocean gliders. Improve the capability for assessing hypoxia and its impacts by prioritizing observation systems (platforms and gliders) measuring dissolved oxygen in coastal waters.

Status/Planned Action:

The 2011 Budget supports these efforts.

Selected Reference(s):

UNESCO 2005, *An Implementation Strategy for the Coastal Module of the Global Ocean Observing System*, GOOS Report No. 148; IOC Information Documents Series N°1217. The document is also available at http://ioc.unesco.org/goos/docs/doclist.htm

IGOS, *A Coastal Theme for the IGOS Partnership-For the Monitoring of our Environment from Space and from Earth*, Paris, UNESCO 2006, 60p

Sandifer, P., C. Sotka, D. Garrison, and V. Fay, *Interagency Oceans and Human Health Research Implementation Plan: A Prescription for the Future*, Interagency Working Group on Harmful Algal Blooms, Hypoxia, and Human Health of the Joint Subcommittee on Ocean Science and Technology, Washington DC, 2007

Griffis, R.B., R. L. Feldman, N. K. Beller-Simms, K. E. Osgood, and N. Cyr (editors): Incorporating Climate Change into NOAA's Stewardship Responsibilities for Living Marine Resources and Coastal Ecosystems: A Strategy for Progress, U.S. Department of Commerce National Oceanic and Atmospheric Administration National Marine Fisheries Service NOAA Technical Memorandum NMFS-F/SPO-95 December 2008

Earth Radiation Budget/Total Solar Irradiance:

The Earth's radiation budget is in balance between absorbed incoming energy from the sun and outgoing thermal energy from the Earth. Solar radiant energy is the major driver of the Earth's climate. The input of energy from the sun is understood increasingly well since we began measuring total solar irradiance from space in 1978. This measurement is the main driver of climate and the only source of climate variability that we have been able to measure. The amount of radiation leaving the Earth through the complex system of clouds, aerosols, atmospheric constituents, oceans, ice, and land surfaces provides a quantitative, system level check of global climate model results. Accurate measurements of the Earth's radiation budget have also been made since 1978 from satellite instruments designed for this purpose. In addition, surface measurement networks are essential to improving our understanding of both radiative and non-radiative forcing of climate.

Recommendations:

NASA should continue plans to launch Glory in 2010, a mission to observe aerosols and total solar irradiance, the latter with a continuation of the SOlar Radiation and Climate Experiment (SORCE) Total Irradiance Monitor (TIM) instrument. NOAA and NASA should continue development and remanifestation of Clouds and the Earth's Radiant Energy System (CERES) for Earth radiation budget data on NPP and JPSS, and launch the remanifested Total Solar Irradiance Sensor (TSIS) as soon as a launch vehicle has been identified by the JPSS program. Maintain and expand the AErosol RObotic NETwork (AERONET) and the Department of Energy's Atmospheric Radiation Measurement (ARM) Climate Research Facility (ACRF) ground networks.

NOAA and DOE should continue their support of the Baseline Surface Radiation Network, the Surface Energy Budget Network, and other surface radiation measurements to provide independent information on trends, distributions, and fluxes of radiant energy, and to aid in validating satellite retrievals. International activities should be continued to ensure global coverage and consistency of measurements.

Status:

CERES is now scheduled to fly on the first JPSS satellite; options for carrying TSIS on orbit are under review. The 2011 Budget supports these NASA and NOAA efforts.

Selected Reference(s):

National Research Council, *Ensuring the Climate Record from the NPOESS and GOES-R Spacecraft: Elements of a Strategy to Recover Measurement Capabilities Lost in Program Restructuring*, National Academies Press, Washington DC, 2008

National Research Council, *Radiative Forcing of Climate Change; Expanding the Concept and Addressing Uncertainties*, Report by the Board on Atmospheric Sciences and Climate (BASC), to the National Academy of Sciences, The National Academies Press, Washington DC, 2005

DOE/SC-ARM-0803, *Contributions of the Atmospheric Radiation measurement (ARM) Program and the ARM Climate Research Facility to the U.S. Climate Change Science Program*, September 2008

Augustine J., E.G. Dutton, T. Meyers, J. Michalsky, *Scientific Rationale for the Placement of Sites to Monitor the Surface Energy Budget for Climate Applications*, NOAA Technical Memorandum OAR GMD-17, October 2006

Fires:

To support wildland fire management and protect lives and property, there is a need for frequent satellite surveillance coupled with tactical thermal remote sensing to support real-time fire incident management. National assets including *in situ* programs, satellite sensors, aerial vehicles (manned and unmanned) are required. Ongoing programs such as the *in situ* Forest Inventory and Analysis (FIA) program and Landscape Fire and Resource Management Planning Tools Project (LANDFIRE) to measure and estimate surface and canopy fuel parameters, and other interagency programs designed to measure specific fire effects need to be continued and follow-on efforts need to be planned and developed. For communities at risk from wildfire the use of airborne Light Detecting and Ranging (LiDAR) to map fuels (vegetation and structures) can provide fine resolution data for risk assessment and fire behavior model inputs. Coarse-resolution satellite sensors such as the Moderate Resolution Imaging Spectroradiometer (MODIS) have been providing forecasting functions for fire dangers as well as real-time fire occurrence reports and information to aid in the deployment of aerial assets. In fact, for Alaska and many other remote areas of the world, MODIS-derived fire boundaries are the only source of tactical information for the wildland fire community. In more heavily populated regions, and for large wildfire incidents, manned aircraft and field teams on the ground are the primary data sources used to manage active fire perimeters, hotspots, and fire spread. Processes are underway to add real-time fire product delivery and unmanned aircraft to the fire manager's toolbox.

Recommendations:

Ensure the VIIRS instrument is sufficient for maintaining the fire climate data record. A spatial resolution of 100 meters for visible/infrared bands and 500 meters for the thermal bands, with coverage every 6 hours is highly desirable. Develop

LDCM data at a 30 m spatial resolution. Through the U.S. Department of Agriculture (USDA), support the continued development and deployment of *in situ* fire monitoring capabilities and sensors for manned and unmanned aerial platforms supporting tactical fire management and fire research.

Status:

The FY11 Budget proposes a $679 million increase for the JPSS program (including VIIRS development).

Selected Reference(s):

Office of the Federal Coordinator for Meteorological Services and Supporting Research, *National Wildland Fire Weather: A Summary of User Needs and Issues*, Joint Action Group (JAG) for the National Wildland Fire Weather Needs Assessment (NWFWNA), 3 July 2007

United States Department of Agriculture Forest Service, FS-865, *Forest Inventory and Analysis Strategic Plan*, January 2007

GeoHazard and Deformation Monitoring:

High-resolution digital topography is a key unmet need for many of the disasters addressed by the CENR Subcommittee for Disaster Reduction (SDR). Changes in the Earth's surface, or deformation, serve as important indicators of earthquakes, volcanic eruptions and landslides. Currently there is no domestic capability to monitor deformation. Our aging and sparsely distributed seismic network infrastructure should be refreshed and expanded if we are to provide adequate warning of earthquakes and volcanic eruptions in the United States. Currently only 5 of 26 major metropolitan regions that are at-risk for major damage in an earthquake have seismic networks that can adequately support earthquake emergency response. Engineers do not have the data needed to refine earthquake resistant building designs. Most lifelines (e.g., electrical power, communications, transportation, etc.) are not adequately monitored for potential earthquake damage. The National Research Council estimated that the benefit/cost ratio for improved seismic monitoring is approximately 10:1; many national organizations have called for full implementation of an Advanced National Seismic System (ANSS) to address this significant monitoring gap.

Recommendations:

Surface Deformation: If necessary, the lidar and radar instruments on DESDynI can be flown on different platforms. The L-Band Interferometric Synthetic Aperture Radar (InSAR) will provide surface deformation measurements. Sustain the geodetic monitoring capabilities of the National Science Foundation's Earthscope program.

Earthquakes and Tsunami: Implement the Advanced National Seismic System (ANSS), and sustain the capabilities of the Global Seismographic Network (GSN). Expand the number of offshore seismic nodes in the Ocean Observatories Initiative (OOI).

Volcanic Activity: The U.S. Geological Survey is implementing the National Volcano Early Warning System (NVEWS); NVEWS activities continue in the 2011 Budget after formulation of an implementation plan in 2010.

Geodetic Reference Frame: Sustain the U.S. supported capabilities of the Global Navigation Satellite System (GNSS) network.

Status:

The 2011 Budget provides an augmentation over previous budget plans for NASA to launch the Deformation, Ecosystem Structure, and Dynamics of Ice (DESDynI) mission in 2017. It also provides an increase to USGS to invest in the Advanced National Seismic System and National Volcano Early Warning System.

Selected Reference(s):

Subcommittee for Disaster Reduction, 2005, *Grand Challenges in Disaster Reduction*, Committee on Environment and Natural Resources, 21p

National Research Council, *Earth Science and Applications from Space: National Imperatives for the Next Decade and Beyond*, National Academies Press, Washington DC, 2007

European Space Agency (ESA), 2004, *IGOS Geohazards Theme Report*. http://www.igosgeohazards.org

Helz, R., and J. Gaynor, 2007, *Reducing Loss of Life and Property from Disasters: A Societal Benefit Area of the Strategic Plan for U.S. Integrated Earth Observation System (IEOS)*, Open-File Report 2007-1147

National Research Council (NRC), Committee on the Economic Benefits of Improved Seismic Monitoring, 2005, *Improved Seismic Monitoring-Improved Decision Making: Assessing the Value of Reduced Uncertainty*, http://www.nap.edu/-catalog/11327.html

Gravity:

Gravity measurement and monitoring is of significant importance for a variety of applications, including monitoring ice sheet mass and accurate vertical positioning. Direct measurement of ice mass is now possible from the joint German Aerospace-NASA gravity measuring mission called the Gravity Recovery and Climate Experiment (GRACE). Time-varying gravity measurements from GRACE provide the best means for determining the partitioning of water stored among the oceans, continents, and ice sheets and glaciers. In particular, direct measurements of changes in ice sheet mass every 10 days with a high degree of accuracy (±5%) provide diagnostic data on ice sheet dynamics that are linked directly to understanding sea level rise.

Gravity measurements also provide the only means of mapping the ocean floor bathymetry on a large scale, and determining the partitioning of water storage among continents, oceans, and ice sheets and glaciers. Gravity methods are also needed to measure and monitor ground-water storage. The current Gravity Recovery and Climate Experiment (GRACE) satellites were launched in 2002 and are already past the end of their planned life. In addition, aerial and ground based gravity measurements provide the high resolution detail necessary for accurate geoid modeling, which is critical to vertical positioning. NOAA's Gravity for the Redefinition of the American Vertical Datum (GRAV-D) project will connect these measurements to satellite observations to provide highly accurate heights critical for monitoring coastal land change in relation to the water. Knowledge of the land movement is absolutely necessary for determining local sea level change and the impact to coastal communities. Furthermore, accurate monitoring of elevations is necessary to properly keep floodplains up to date for the mitigation of flood hazards from extreme weather events.

Recommendations:

Sustain observations of the time-varying gravity field from the Gravity Recovery and Climate Experiment (GRACE-1) and launch GRACE-FO in 2016 ("FO" for "Follow On"), a gap-filler mission with the same capabilities and characteristics as GRACE-1. NASA should plan for a follow-on GRACE-2 mission in 2020 to continue estimating changes in ocean mass, terrestrial water storage, and ice sheet mass. Support NOAA's Gravity for the Redefinition of the American Vertical Datum (GRAV-D) project. The goal is to collect gravity data for a new national vertical datum by 2023 which will allow improvement in elevations through Global Positioning System (GPS) technology to an accuracy of ~2 centimeters compared to 2 meters today, with profound implications for all activities relying on accurate heights. Sustain NOAA's Deep-ocean Assessment and Reporting of Tsunamis (DART) network of ocean bottom pressure recorders. These data are crucial for calibrating GRACE gravity field measurements.

Status/Planned Actions:

The 2011 Budget provides funding for GRACE FO to be launched in 2016. NOAA proposes to improve the DART network in the 2011 Budget, and continue the GRAV-D FY10 initiative.

Selected Reference(s):

National Research Council, *Earth Science and Applications from Space: National Imperatives for the Next Decade and Beyond*, National Academies Press, Washington DC, 2007

Luthcke, S.B., D.D. Rowlands, J.J. McCarthy, H.J. Zwally, A Arendt, D Hall, J.P. Boy, and F.G Lemoine, Recent Land Ice Mass Changes Determined From GRACE Mascon Solution, Geophysical Research Abstracts, Vol. 10, EGU2008-A-04338, EGU General Assembly, 2008

http://www.ngs.noaa.gov/GRAV-D/GRAV-D_v2007_12_19.pdf

http://nctr.pmel.noaa.gov/Dart/

Greenhouse Gases:

Greenhouse gases are trace constituents of our atmosphere, but have a major impact upon Earth's climate through their absorption of outgoing longwave radiation. The principal greenhouse gases are water vapor, carbon dioxide, methane, nitrous oxide, ozone, and the chlorofluorocarbons. This past year marked the 50th anniversary of Charles David Keeling's Mauna Loa carbon dioxide record, the longest continuous record of atmospheric carbon dioxide measurements, and which continues as part of the NOAA's global cooperative air sampling network. NOAA's data collection effort has broadened to include other greenhouse gases and serves as the foundation of our understanding of greenhouse gas concentrations and the global carbon cycle. The AmeriFlux network, established in 1996, provides continuous observations of ecosystem level exchanges of CO_2, water, energy and momentum spanning diurnal, synoptic, seasonal, and interannual time scales and is currently composed of sites from North America, Central America, and South America. Today, precise ground-based and air-based measurements such as these are the main tool for scientists monitoring the rise of atmospheric carbon dioxide concentrations. Comparisons of these data with carbon dioxide emission rates from fossil fuel combustion, biomass burning and other human activities tell us that only about half of the carbon dioxide released into the atmosphere during this period has remained there. The rest has apparently been absorbed by surface "sinks" in the land biosphere or oceans. These measurements also show that, despite the steady long-term growth of carbon dioxide in the atmosphere, the buildup varies dramatically from year to year, even though emissions have increased smoothly. However, the ground-based carbon dioxide monitoring network is currently too sparse to identify the locations of these sinks or tell us what controls changes in their efficiency from year to year. For the past two decades, NOAA has been making efforts to develop a more dense and comprehensive greenhouse gas monitoring network across North America, as part of the USGCRP North American Carbon Program, and has developed an analysis tool for integrating these measurements and translating them into fluxes. Space-based remote sensing of atmospheric carbon dioxide has the potential to deliver additional data needed to resolve many of the uncertainties in the spatial and temporal variability of carbon sources and sinks. Many studies have shown that space-based measurements with the needed precision, temporal and spatial resolution, together with the highly accurate and appropriately distributed surface measurements, will reduce uncertainties in CO_2 sources and sinks due to uniform and global sampling. However, satellite measurements of CO_2 and other greenhouse gases, though hopeful, are in their infancy and will require on-going validation and comparison with ground and air-based networks (e.g., NOAA's global and North American networks and TCCCON) to ensure that biases are not being introduced. Consistency among ground, air, and satellite measurements is paramount and must be tied to World Calibration Scales and be comparable across the globe.

Better carbon cycle monitoring capabilities and insight on the underlying dynamics controlling atmosphere exchange with the land and ocean reservoirs are needed as society begins to discuss active management of the global carbon system. Understanding the global carbon cycle depends on monitoring the stock and flow of carbon in the oceans, on land, and in the atmosphere, as well as the air-sea CO_2 exchange.

Recommendations:

NASA should launch a replacement for the Orbiting Carbon Observatory (OCO, lost in February 2009) in 2013 and build a spare OCO instrument for possible launch in 2015-2017. The outcome of NASA's OCO mission should be used to evaluate the technical approach for the next generation greenhouse gas sensors. The OCO mission can provide data products with the precision, temporal and spatial resolution, and coverage needed to characterize the variability of CO_2 sources and sinks on regional spatial scales and seasonal to inter-annual timescales. These should be tied to accurate *in situ* surface sensor measurements (e.g., the global cooperative air sampling network, the Total Column Carbon Network (TCCN) of ground-based high-resolution spectrometers, and the Ameriflux Network). These surface sensor networks should be continued and improved.

NASA should plan to evaluate different laser sounder instruments for measuring atmospheric CO_2, as called for in the Active Sensing of CO_2 Emission over Nights, Days, and Seasons (ASCENDS) Decadal Survey mission. The laser CO_2 sounder instruments could complement OCO and provide a great density of measurements through their day and night duty cycle. NASA may consider additional testing that could include aircraft or other platforms to mitigate risk. NASA should also undertake research to monitor CH_4 from space.

Support NOAA's ground and air-based measurements of greenhouse gases to provide accurate, independent measures of the trends, distributions and fluxes of CO_2 and other greenhouse gases (e.g., N_2O, CH_4, halocarbons), to aid in verifying satellite retrievals, and to provide needed information on trace gases for refining transport models and emission sources. Support NOAA's measurements of carbon and dissolved oxygen from ocean carbon survey vessels and on a subset of the Argo float array to further understand carbon sequestration and carbon cycle-climate feedbacks and ocean acidification. Support ship-based efforts to systematically collect full water column data on ocean carbon, such as the U.S. Global Ocean Carbon and Repeat Hydrography Program.

Support the interagency AmeriFlux network that provides continuous observations of ecosystem level exchanges of CO_2, water, energy and momentum spanning diurnal, synoptic, seasonal, and interannual time scales and is currently composed of sites from North America, Central America, and South America.

NOAA and NASA should continue their support of international coordinating mechanisms through WMO (particularly Global Atmospheric Watch), Global Climate Observing System and its supporting panels, and the intergovernmental Group on Earth Observations (GEO) to ensure that global observing systems are coordinated and comparable and to maximize benefit of international observing systems.

Status:

The 2011 Budget proposes to launch the OCO-2 in 2013 and proposes $171 million in FY 2011 for the mission.

Selected Reference(s):

Miller, C., D. Crisp, P.L. DeCola, S.C. Olsen, J.T. Randerson, A.M. Michalak, A. Alkhaled, P. Rayner, D. J. Jacob, et al. Precision requirements for space-based XCO_2 data, J. Geophys. Res., 112, D10314, 2007

Orbiting Carbon Observatory information at: http://oco.jpl.nasa.gov/

Washenfelder, R.A., G.C. Toon, J.-F. Blavier, Z. Yang, N. T. Allen, P. O. Wennberg, S. A. Vay, D. M. Matross, and B. C. Daube , *Carbon dioxide column abundances at the Wisconsin Tall Tower site*, J. Geophys. Res., 111, D22305, 2006, doi:10.1029/2006JD007154

IPCC AR4 WGI Chapter 7

http://public.ornl.gov/ameriflux/

Landscape Characterization/Vegetation:

The continued and consistent monitoring of vegetation photosynthetic capacity, land cover, the impacts of droughts and floods, and understanding phenology are critical to understanding earth's biosphere. Vegetation structure characterizations, such as canopy height, stand diameter, and canopy bulk density, have many applications including: 1/ calculating biomass and hence carbon sequestration; 2/ estimating fuel loads for fire prevention, planning, and modeling; 3/ understanding succession stages of vegetation communities and impacts of climate change; and 4/ informing land management decisions. Presently, some vegetation applications of space-borne remote sensing remain in the research domain although operational spaceborne data are clearly needed to support policy, environmental, and land management decision-making.

Scientists have been able to exploit data from sensors that were not intended for observations of the landscape, such as the Advanced Very High Resolution Radiometer (AVHRR) with its 28-year record, and cross calibrate them with Landsat with its 38-year record and the Moderate Resolution Imaging Spectroradiometer (MODIS) with its 9-year record. The AVHRR-MODIS time series will be continued by the Visible/Infrared Imager Radiometer Suite (VIIRS) instruments on the Joint Polar Satellite System (JPSS) while the Landsat record will be continued by the NASA-USGS Landsat Data Continuity Mission (LDCM).

Supporting sustainable agricultural practices and long-term ecosystem management requires a high degree of understanding of constantly changing complex conditions on the ground and as the result of ever-increasing socio-economic demands, pressures, and interactions. Understanding localized cycles of causes and effects, as well as mitigation strategies that optimize agricultural and forest production, and continued provision of ecosystem services, requires long-term, *in situ*, and remote sensing observations. For food security, producers require continual feedback on within-season production progress for remedial actions when factors such as pests, water, nutrient deficiency, or drought intervene to limit production.

Recommendations:

Continue improvements to the Visible/Infrared Imagery Radiometer Suite (VIIRS) instrument scheduled to be deployed on NPP and JPSS. Evaluate an operational moderate-resolution satellite program that would meet the land imaging needs of U.S. civil agencies and society, in accordance with the OSTP-led Future of Land Imaging Interagency Working Group's recommendations in the 2007 document "A Plan for a U.S. National Land Imaging Program." Planning for Landsat-9 is being undertaken by the USGS and NASA, in cooperation with other stake-holders. This planning, however, must look beyond Landsat 9 and lay out requirements for an operational Landsat program. Recommendations for future Landsat-like instruments include a spatial resolution of at most 20 meters, at least a 5-day repeat cycle, increased daily acquisition rates, and possibly additional visual shortwave infrared and thermal infrared spectral bands. Additional higher spatial-resolution imagery will still be required to understand field-level conditions. These data could be acquired from commercial sources, or by the Federal government if the commercial sources do not meet requirements. NASA and USGS are moving forward toward an LDCM launch in 2012. NASA plans to launch the Deformation, Ecosystem Structure, and Dynamics of Ice (DESDynI) mission in 2017 to provide canopy height and structure measurements. DESDynI is an important carbon cycle climate mission for providing forest biomass and carbon globally. As such, it will be key to identifying the forest carbon sink of ~30% of current global CO_2 emissions. In addition, it will provide laser altimetry and SAR data from ice sheets. If necessary, the DESDynI lidar and DESDynI radar could be separated and flown on different platforms. Sustain the National Agriculture Imagery Program (NAIP) and the follow-on program Imagery for the Nation (IFTN). The 2011 Budget continues NAIP.

Status/Planned Actions:

The 2011 Budget requests a $679 million increase for the JPSS program that includes continued development of VIIRS toward a target delivery date of FY 2013. It also requests a $13.35 million increase to the USGS to accommodate ground system requirements changes for LDCM.

Selected Reference(s):

Future of Land Imaging Interagency Working Group, *A Plan for a U.S. National Land Imaging Program*, August 2007

Geographical Sciences Committee, National Research Council, *Contributions of Land Remote Sensing for Decisions about Food Security and Human Health: Workshop Report*, National Academies Press, Washington DC, 2007

National Research Council, *Earth Science and Applications from Space: National Imperatives for the Next Decade and Beyond*, National Academies Press, Washington DC, 2007

National Agriculture Imaging Program (NAIP) and the Imagery for the Nation

http://www.nsgic.org/hottopics/naip_briefing_0308.pdf

http://www.nsgic.org/hottopics/imageryforthenation.cfm

Anderson M., and W. Kustas, Thermal Remote Sensing of Drought and
Evapotranspiration, EOS, Transactions, American Geophysical Union, EOS Vol. 89,
No. 26, 24 June 2008, p 233-240

Ocean Color:

Today's satellite ocean color radiometry data form the backbone of assessing primary
productivity and carbon cycling in the ocean, providing fisheries and integrated
ecosystem assessments, and measuring and monitoring coastal and ocean habitat changes,
and climate impacts. With the current record of more than 12 years of climate-research
quality ocean color observations, it is now possible to identify interannual variability in
marine ecosystems and to start discerning long-term trends. These measurements are
collected by the Sea-viewing Wide Field-of-view Sensor (SeaWiFS) mission, which was
launched on August 1, 1997 and, being beyond its expected lifetime, has experienced
"outages" during which data are not available. Similarly, the Moderate Resolution Imaging
Spectroradiometer (MODIS) instrument on Aqua was launched in 2002 and, though
currently in good health, is also past its expected lifetime. The follow-on ocean color
instruments are the VIIRS instruments on NPP and JPSS. It is presently unclear if the
first VIIRS sensor to be deployed will have the full capability of SeaWiFS, however,
subsequent VIIRS units are expected to meet, if not exceed, SeaWiFS's capability.

The National Academy of Sciences, National Research Council Committee on
Assessing Requirements for Sustained Ocean Color Research and Operations has
begun a study on the Nation's economic and societal need and associated observational
requirements for continuing a U.S. ocean color capability in space after the SeaWiFS and
MODIS capabilities are no longer available. The pre-publication version of the report
from this study is anticipated to be available in February 2011, with the final report
published the following June.

Recommendations:

NOAA and NASA continue to pursue international partnerships (e.g., ESA, JAXA,
ISRO) to provide risk mitigation strategies for ocean color measurements. Should VIIRS
not meet ocean color requirements, investigate improvements to VIIRS to meet this
requirement. Explore whether the ocean color component of NASA's Aerosol-Cloud-

Ecosystems (ACE) Decadal Survey mission could function as a potential complement to VIIRS. When released, the results of the National Research Council Committee on Assessing Requirements for Sustained Ocean Color Research and Operations study should be used to refine the satellite strategy. Sustain the NASA-NOAA's Marine Optical Buoy (MOBY) program and the AERONET-Maritime Aerosol Network.

Status/Planned Actions:

The 2011 Budget provides an augmentation over previous budget plans for NASA to begin development of the Pre-Aerosol, Clouds, and Ocean Ecosystem (PACE) mission for launch in 2018. It also includes a $679 million increase in NOAA for the JPSS program (including VIIRS development), and sustains the MOBY and AERONET programs.

Selected Reference(s):

National Research Council, *Earth Science and Applications from Space: National Imperatives for the Next Decade and Beyond*, National Academies Press, Washington DC, 2007

http://www.star.nesdis.noaa.gov/sod/orad/mot/moce/overview.html

Information about the AERONET Maritime Aerosol Network can be found at: http://aeronet.gsfc.nasa.gov/new_web/maritime_aerosol_network.html

Ocean Surface Vector Winds:

Winds over the ocean are the largest source of momentum for the ocean surface, and as such they affect the full range of ocean movement—from individual surface waves to complete current systems. Ocean surface vector winds (OSVW) also play a key role in regulating the earth's water and energy cycles by modulating air-sea exchanges of heat, moisture, gases (such as carbon dioxide), and particulates. This modulation regulates the interaction between the atmosphere and the ocean, which establishes and maintains both global and regional climates. Furthermore, OSVW are required to compute air-sea fluxes and are used in numerical modeling of the ocean and atmosphere for weather and wave forecasts, biophysical interactions and climate studies. As such, characterization and quantification of the role of the global ocean as a planetary heat and carbon sink depends on the accurate representation of the global OSVW.

NASA's polar orbiting Quick Scatterometer (QuikSCAT) satellite had provided over ten years of nearly continuous ocean surface vector winds (OSVW) data before its failure in November 2009. These measurements proved to be of important value for climate studies and revolutionized operational marine weather warnings, analyses, and forecasting within National Weather Service (NWS) offices. QuikSCAT provided critical wind data that enabled NWS to significantly improve the accuracy of hurricane force wind warnings in offshore regions in the Atlantic and Pacific oceans for non-tropical ocean storms, and for tropical storms in the Pacific Ocean. Warnings over offshore regions of the Atlantic and Pacific Oceans are often determined solely by QuikSCAT data. These winds were also used in combination with boundary layer models to determine a sea level pressure field and estimate the central pressure of cyclones and as a diagnostic to determine the accuracy of numerical model analyses and short term forecasts for ocean cyclones, including those potentially threatening to land.

In June 2006, NOAA conducted an OSVW operational requirements workshop, which documented the impact that OSVW data from QuikSCAT has on NWS operations and need for a more advanced satellite OSVW capability. The NRC Decadal Survey recommended that NOAA, the operational satellite data provider, establish a sustained satellite OSVW capability. NOAA has also been actively studying QuikSCAT follow-on mission options.

Recommendations:

NOAA and NASA should establish a sustained source for OSVW information. Explore international partnerships as cost-effective opportunities to sustain this capability. Maintain the airborne Stepped Frequency Microwave Radiometer (SFMR) capability aboard the Hurricane Hunter WC-130J and NOAA's P-3 aircraft, and support follow-on technologies such as the Hurricane Intensity Radiometer (HIRAD) which shows promise to provide improved prediction of hurricane intensity and will provide measurements through precipitation. Maintain the existing array of fixed and drifting surface data buoys.

Status/Planned Actions:

The FY11 Budget partially supports these efforts.

Selected Reference(s):

National Research Council, *Earth Science and Applications from Space: National Imperatives for the Next Decade and Beyond*, National Academies Press, Washington DC, 2007

Chang, P. S. and Z. Jelenek, 2006, NOAA Operational Ocean Surface Vector Winds Requirements Workshop Report, 52 pp. Available online at: http://manati.star.nesdis. noaa.gov/SVW_nextgen/SVW_workshop_report_final.pdf

Jelenak, Z. and P. S. Chang, 2008, NOAA Operational Satellite Ocean Surface Vector Winds -QuikSCAT Follow-On Mission: User Impact Study Report, 90 pp. Available online at: http://manati.star.nesdis.noaa.gov/SVW_nextgen/QFO_user_impact_ study_final.pdf

Gaston, R. and E. Rodriguez, 2008, QuikSCAT Follow-On Concept Study, 60pp. Available online at: http://winds.jpl.nasa.gov/publications/QFO_ MissionConceptReport_JPL_08-18_2.pdf

Precipitation:

One of the critical components of the Earth's hydrological cycle is precipitation, affecting virtually every environmental issue. In many respects, precipitation is truly the centerpiece of our planet's hydrological cycle, and understanding it is crucial to unraveling many of the uncertainties about the water cycle, climate change and its impacts. Careful analysis of rainfall trends in amount and regional patterns are likely to produce important scientific breakthroughs in understanding climate change impacts on rainfall patterns. Over the ocean, which covers roughly 70% of the Earth's surface, space-based measurements are critical as the sole data source, whereas over land, the coupling of satellite data with ground-based observations provides the most useful data.

Recommendations:

NASA should launch the joint U.S. and Japan Global Precipitation Measurement (GPM) mission to minimize the likelihood of a gap in the rainfall measurement record provided by the Tropical Rainfall Measurement Mission (TRMM). Sustain support for NOAA's U.S. Climate Reference Network (USCRN) and continue work on NOAA's Surface Energy Budget Network (SEBN) and the Historical Climatology Network-Modernization

(HCN-M) to provide ground-based precipitation measurements. Maintain the Nation's NEXRAD network and move toward a dual polarization capability for NEXRAD. Dual polarization will provide the capability to discriminate between precipitation types and provide a significant improvement in estimating rainfall rates. Ensure continued support of the Department of Energy's Atmospheric Radiation Measurement (ARM) Climate Research Facility (ACRF) ground networks. ACRF's addition of new scanning precipitation radars as well as scanning dual frequency cloud radars provides a strong capability for characterizing cloud properties and linking with precipitation processes.

Status/Planned Actions:

The 2011 Budget provides an augmentation over previous budget plans for NASA to launch the GPM mission in 2013. The 2011 Budget proposes additional NEXRAD funding for acquisition and deployment of dual polarization technology.

Selected Reference(s):

National Research Council, *Earth Science and Applications from Space: Urgent Needs and Opportunities to Serve the Nation*, National Academies Press, Washington DC, 2005

Information about the U.S. Historical Climate Network can be found at:
http://cdiac.ornl.gov/epubs/ndp/ushcn/background.html

Information about the U.S. Climate Reference Network can be found at:
http://www.ncdc.noaa.gov/oa/climate/uscrn/

Sea Level:

Since the beginning of high-accuracy satellite altimetry in the early 1990s, global mean sea-level has been observed by altimeters to be rising at a rate of 3.1 millimeters per year from 1993 to 2008, roughly 50% faster than the tide-gauge-measured rate over the past century. About 60% of the sea-level rise is due to thermal expansion of the oceans; the other 40% contribution is from melting glaciers and ice sheets. Sea level measurements play an important role in monitoring global climate change and understanding and responding to threats to our coastal regions. Space-based altimetry can also be used to assess the strength of hurricanes. The Ocean Surface Topography Mission (also known as Jason-2) was launched in June 2008, replacing the original

Jason-1 satellite which collected sea level data since December 2001. Jason-2 will reach the end of its nominal life in 2013. The Jason missions are a partnership between NOAA, NASA and the French space agency, Centre National d'Etudes Spatiales (CNES), and the European Organization for the Exploitation of Meteorological Satellites. Complementary *in situ* temperature measurements from ocean profilers, such as the current Argo float array are needed to understand the underlying density contributions to sea level rise, and continental ice measurements from satellites, such GRACE and CryoSat, are needed to understand the mass contributions.

Recommendations:

The sea level rise problem requires a comprehensive observing system approach, built around the measurement of sea level and the contributions to sea level change from both mass and density changes. NOAA and EUMETSAT should continue their Jason partnership by extending the current generation of altimeters with Jason-3, scheduled for launch in 2013, and Jason-CS, a series of advanced follow-on missions beginning in 2018. NOAA should also continue, working in collaboration with other space agencies through the CEOS Ocean Surface Topography Virtual Constellation to ensure maximum benefit from the set of international sea level altimeter missions. In conjunction with the Jason program, it is important to maintain the 220+ sea-level tide gauges, the U.S. portion of the integrated Global Ocean Observing System (GOOS), and incorporate Global Positioning System (GPS) capability. Tide gauge observations are essential for calibrating altimeter observations and, in some cases, provide a long (100 year) record useful for interpreting current trends. To determine the mass contributions from the melting of grounded ice and other continental sources, NASA should continue the GRACE gravity measurements (see Gravity Section), launch Ice, Cloud, and land Elevation Satellite-2 (ICESat-2) in 2015, proceed with the Landsat Data Continuity Mission (LDCM) and DESDynI radar mission to measure outlet glacier velocities, and proceed with the DESDynI lidar mission to continue beyond ICESat-2 crucial altimetry of ice sheets. And, to monitor and understand the density contributions to sea level change, it is important that NOAA continue supporting the Argo float array to monitor heat in the upper ocean, add a capability to provide deep ocean (>2000 down to 5000 m) profile measurements, and deploy real-time-reporting ocean-bottom-mounted arrays to monitor changing ocean circulation and global heat transport.

Status/Planned Actions:

The FY11 Budget fully funds Jason-3 and requests an increase of $4 million for the GOOS program.

Selected Reference(s):

Wilson, W.S. et al. 2010. Observing Systems Needed to Address Sea-Level Rise and Variability, pp 376-401 in *Understanding Sea-level Rise and Variability*, J. Church, P.L. Woodworth, T. Aarup and W.S. Wilson (eds), John Wiley

Soil moisture:

Soil moisture data can greatly improve how the understanding and representation of the water, energy and carbon cycles in global models of weather and climate, resulting in significant advances in long-range weather and seasonal forecasts. Global soil moisture measurements can provide improved early warning and decision support for droughts, better predictions of agricultural productivity, and improved flood forecasts, especially in the developing world. It is also a key indicator for heat stress, waterborne infectious disease, disease vectors, zoonotic diseases, permafrost, and freeze/thaw for water cycle processes. Despite this significant promise there is currently no integrated national or global network of sufficient density to measure it. Existing surface networks such as the U.S. Climate Reference Network (USCRN) and the USDA's Soil Climate Analysis Network (SCAN) should be continued to ensure a continuous and homogeneous data record.

Recommendations:

The European Space Agency has recently launched and is successfully operating the Soil Moisture and Ocean Salinity (SMOS) mission. Proceed with the NASA Soil Moisture Active-Passive (SMAP) mission to augment this data record. Sustain NOAA's U.S. Climate Reference Network (USCRN) and USDA's Soil Climate Analysis Network (SCAN) *in situ* soil moisture networks. Work towards implementing the 2008 National Research Council recommendation of a national, real-time network of soil moisture observations at approximately 3000 sites.

Status/Planned Actions:

The 2011 Budget provides an augmentation over previous budget plans for NASA to launch the SMAP mission in 2014.

The FY11 Budget sustains the USCRN and SCAN programs.

Selected Reference(s):

National Research Council, *Earth Science and Applications from Space: National Imperatives for the Next Decade and Beyond*, National Academies Press, Washington DC, 2007

National Research Council, *Observing Weather and Climate From the Ground Up: A Nationwide Network of Networks*, The National Academies Press, Washington, DC, 2008

Soil Climate Analysis Network (SCAN): http://www.wcc.nrcs.usda.gov/wsf/wsf.html

Solar Wind and Magnetic Storms:

The sun's activities, such as solar flares and coronal mass ejections, affect the Earth's geomagnetic field. The resulting geomagnetic storms have the capability to disable satellites, disrupt Global Positioning System (GPS), induce large currents in the Nation's power grids, and disrupt oil and gas pipeline control. NOAA and the U.S. Air Force provide space weather forecasts based on ground-based and satellite observing systems operated by NOAA, DOD, NASA, USGS, and numerous international partners. Our ability to provide advanced warning of these storms to satellite operators and power grid and pipeline managers is currently threatened due to the age of a research satellite stationed in the solar wind that is being relied on for operational alerts and warnings. NASA's Advanced Composition Explorer (ACE) satellite, which maintains a continuous position between the Earth and the sun, was launched in 1997 and is currently eight years past its design life. This satellite provides the Nation's only real-time measurements of the energetic particles coming from the sun (the "solar wind").

Important, long-term observations of magnetic activity at the Earth's surface provide baseline calibration and tracking on magnetic storms, with applications in power grid management, precision drilling and elsewhere. While the ACE satellite is important for early detection of solar winds in time to provide alerts of magnetic storms; in a complementary role, the U.S. Geological Survey (USGS) network of 14 ground-based geomagnetic observatories are essential for monitoring the effects of magnetic disturbances at the Earth's surface, where they impact our human activities. These observatories are currently in need of modernization to meet the needs of data users such as the U.S. Air Force, NOAA and others. The government should continue to explore commercial alternatives to government missions to satisfy national requirements to observe coronal mass ejections, solar winds, and geomagnetic storms.

Recommendations:

Refurbish the Deep Space Climate Observatory (DSCOVR) satellite and its solar wind sensors to replace the Advanced Composition Explorer (ACE) capability. USGS should modernize the network of ground-based geomagnetic observatories.

Status/Planned Action:

The 2011 Budget provides $9.5 million for the DSCOVR mission, and $3.7 million to Constellation Observing System for Meteorology, Ionosphere, and Climate (COSMIC-2) Mission, a joint US-Taiwan mission to continue access to GPS radio occultation measurements which has proven extremely useful for space weather and meteorological weather improvements.

Selected Reference(s):

National Research Council, *Severe Space Weather Events – Understanding Societal and Economic Impacts*, National Academies Press, Washington DC, 2008

Helz, R., and J. Gaynor, 2007, *Reducing Loss of Life and Property from Disasters: A Societal Benefit Area of the Strategic Plan for U.S. Integrated Earth Observation System (IEOS)*, Open-File Report 2007-1147

National Space Weather Program, *Report of the Assessment Committee for the National Space Weather Program*, FCM-R24-2006, OFCM, Silver Spring, MD, 2006

Water Quality and Quantity:

Management of water resources is challenging because much authority and measurement are delegated to the state, tribal and local levels. The CENR Subcommittee for Water Availability and Quality (SWAQ) recommends a national approach to provide a comprehensive assessment.[22] The WaterSMART plan beginning in FY11 is a great start, as it provides a framework for assessing water availability and use across the Nation. The coarse nature of current sampling is such that important phenomena are missed and/or "averaged out." Additionally, the frequency of sampling needs to be increased. Many locations have only monthly sampling for certain measurements, but really need hourly in some cases. The capability to rapidly detect chemical contaminants and pathogens is also needed.

Recommendations:

Support the modernization of the Nation's 7,000 stream gauges by replacing obsolete telemetry to ensure continued real-time operations and provide more timely information needed for better water management. Consider supplying more opportunities to study large river basins. Investigate and implement new technologies to measure sediment in rivers. Also support the Advisory Committee on Water Information, and the National Water Quality Monitoring Council plan for sustaining and enhancing the Nation's capability to monitor water quality.[23] NASA should continue its observations of gravity fields from GRACE-1 and follow-on gravity missions for ground water storage and ice sheet mass variations. In addition, NOAA and NASA should explore international partnerships to complement JPSS's ability to understand ground water and snow water equivalent (e.g., the Advanced Microwave Scanning Radiometer (AMSR)-2/3 instruments on JAXA's Global Change Observation Mission (GCOM) mission). Continue to improve snow moisture measurements such as SNOwpack TELemetry (SNOTEL) and the NOAA Operational Hydrology Program to increase our understanding of source water from snow and runoff. Support the 2011 WaterSMART water availability and use assessment, which will provide the national framework for assessing water availability.

Status/Planned Actions:

Through ARRA funding, USGS will meet the 2013 deadline of the requirement to upgrade radio transmission on stream gauges. The FY11 Budget supports these efforts through the WaterSMART initiative, which invests an additional $9 million for a multi-year, nationwide study of water availability and use.

Selected Reference(s):

National Science and Technology Council, Committee on Environment and Natural Resources, Subcommittee on Water Availability and Quality, *A Strategy for Federal Science and Technology to Support Water Availability and Quality in the United States*, Sept 2007

U.S. Geological Survey Report to Congress, *Concepts for National Assessment of Water Availability and Use*, Circular 1223, Reston VA, 2002

Advisory Committee on Water Information and the National Water Quality Monitoring Council, *A National Water Quality Monitoring Network for U.S. Coastal Waters and Their Tributaries*, April 2006, http://acwi.gov/monitoring/network/design/

WaterSMART Initiative, http://www.doi.gov/budget/2011/11Hilites/DH019.pdf

SNOTEL: http://www.wcc.nrcs.usda.gov/snotel/

LIST OF ACRONYMS

ACE	Advanced Composition Explorer
ACE	Aerosol-Cloud-Ecosystems
ACRF	Atmospheric Radiation Measurement (ARM) Climate Research Facility (ACRF)
AERONET	AErosol RObotic NETwork
ANSS	Advanced National Seismic System
ARM	Atmospheric Radiation Measurement
AVHRR	Advanced Very High Resolution Radiometer
BSRN	Baseline Surface Radiation Network
CENR	Committee on Environment and Natural Resources
CEOS	Committee on Earth Observation Satellites
CEQ	Council on Environmental Quality
CERES	Clouds and the Earth's Radiant Energy System
DART	Deep-ocean Assessment and Reporting of Tsunamis
DESDynI	Deformation, Ecosystem Structure, and Dynamics of Ice
DOE	Department of Energy
EFR	Experimental Forests and Ranges
EOS	Earth Observing System
EPA	Environmental Protection Agency
EUMETSAT	European Organization for the Exploitation of Meteorological Satellites
FIA	Forest Inventory and Analysis, National Program
GBIF	Global Biodiversity Information Facility
GCOS	Global Climate Observing System
GCOM	Global Change Observation Mission
GEO	Group on Earth Observations
GEOCAPE	Geostationary Coastal and Air Pollution Events
GEOSS	Global Earth Observation System of Systems
GNSS	Global Navigation Satellite System
GSN	Global Seismographic Network
GOES-R	Geostationary Operational Environmental Satellite R-Series

GPM	Global Precipitation Measurement
GPS	Global Positioning System
GRACE	Gravity Recovery And Climate Experiment
GRAV-D	Gravity for the Redefinition of the American Vertical Datum
HCN	Historical Climatology Network
IEOS	Integrated Earth Observation System
IFTN	Imagery for the Nation
InSAR	Interferometric Synthetic Aperture Radar
IOOS	Integrated Ocean Observing System
JAXA	Japan Aerospace Exploration Agency
LANDFIRE	Landscape Fire and Resource Management Planning Tools Project
LDCM	Landsat Data Continuity Mission
Lidar	Light Detection and Ranging
LTER	Long Term Ecological Research
MISR	Multi-angle Imaging SpectroRadiometer
MOBY	Marine Optical Buoy
MODIS	Moderate Resolution Imaging Spectroradiometer
NAIP	National Agriculture Imagery Program
NAMS	National Air Monitoring Stations
NASA	National Aeronautics and Space Agency
NEON	National Ecological Observatory Network
NEPTUNE	North East Pacific Time-integrated Undersea Networked Experiments
NIDIS	National Integrated Drought Information System
NOAA	National Oceanic and Atmospheric Administration
NPOESS	National Polar-orbiting Operational Environmental Satellite System
NPP	NPOESS Preparatory Project
NRC	National Research Council
NRI	National Resources Inventory
NSTC	National Science and Technology Council
NVEWS	National Volcano Early Warning System

NWS	National Weather Service
OCO	Orbiting Carbon Observatory
OMB	Office of Management and Budget
OOI	Ocean Observatories Initiative
OSTM	Ocean Surface Topography Mission (also known as Jason-2)
OSTP	Office of Science and Technology Policy
OSVW	Ocean Surface Vector Winds
PAMS	Photochemical Assessment Monitoring Stations
QuikSCAT	Quick Scatterometer
SAG	Strategic Assessment Group
SBA	Societal Benefit Area
SCAN	Soil Climate Analysis Network
SDR	Subcommittee for Disaster Reduction
SeaWiFS	Sea-viewing Wide Field-of-view Sensor
SEBN	Surface Energy Budget Network
SFMR	Stepped Frequency Microwave Radiometer
SIGEO	Smithsonian Institution Global Earth Observatories
SLAMS	State and Local Air Monitoring Stations
SMAP	Soil Moisture Active-Passive
SNOTEL	SNOwpack TELemetry
SWAQ	Subcommittee on Water Availability and Quality
TCCN	Total Column Carbon Network
TRMM	Tropical Rainfall Measurement Mission
TSIS	Total Solar Irradiance Sensor
USCRN	U.S. Climate Reference Network
USDA	United States Department of Agriculture
USGEO	United States Group on Earth Observations
USGS	Unites States Geological Survey
VIIRS	Visible/Infrared Imagery Radiometer Suite
WMO	World Meteorological Organization

USGEO Strategic Assessment Group (SAG) Writing Team

Co-Chairs:

Philip DeCola – OSTP

Compton J. Tucker – CCSP

Peter A. Wilczynski – NOAA

Co-Authors and Contributors:

Michael R. Babcock – NOAA (OFCM)

Glenn R. Bethel – USDA

E. Ann Davis – NIH

Wanda R. Ferrell – DOE

Jessica Geubtner – NOAA (IOOS)

Randall R. Friedl – NASA

Everett A. Hinkley – USDA Forest Service

Leonard P. Hirsch – Smithsonian Institution

William S. Leith – USGS

John G. Lyon – EPA

Timothy R. Newman – USGS

Graham M. Pugh – DOE

Carolyn M. Vadnais – NOAA

Edward P. Washburn, EPA

Zdenka S. Willis – NOAA (IOOS)

Gregory Withee – NOAA/USGS

ENDNOTES

1   The National Research Council, *Earth Science and Applications from Space: National Imperatives for the Next Decade and Beyond*, The National Academies Press, Washington DC, 2007, p.14

2   Interagency Working Group on Earth Observations, *Strategic Plan for the U.S. Integrated Earth Observation System*, Committee on Environment and Natural Resources, National Science and Technology Council, April 2005

3   United States Department of Defense, *National Defense Strategy*, June 2008; Millennium Ecosystem Assessment: Ecosystems and Human Well Being, Island Press, 2005

4   CENR Joint Subcommittee on Ocean Science and Technology, *Charting the Course for Ocean Science in the Next Decade, An Ocean Research Priorities Plan and Implementation Strategy*, National Science and Technology Council, January 2007. http://ocean.ceq.gov/about/docs/orppfinal.pdf

5   EPA Publication (EPA-454/R-09-002, Feb 2010): *Our Nation's Air - Status and Trends through 2008*, page 3.

6   The National Research Council, *Air Quality Management in the United States*, The National Academies Press, Washington DC, 2004

7   LeQuere C., M.R. Raupach, J.G. Canadell, et al., *Trends in the Sources and Sinks of Carbon Dioxide*, Nature Geoscience, Vol 2, Issue 12, pp. 831-836

8   H. John Heinz III Center for Science Economics and the Environment, *The Hidden Costs of Coastal Hazards: Implications for Risk Assessment and Mitigation*, Island Press, 2000, Washington, D.C.

9   U.S. Geological Survey, *Earthquake Facts and Statistics*, http://neic.usgs.gov/neis/eqlists/eqstats.html

10 U.S. Geological Survey, *Requirements for an Advanced National Seismic System*, U.S. Geological Survey circular 1188, 1999, p.5; Field et al., *Loss estimates for a Puente Hill blind-thrust earthquake in Los Angeles, California*, 2005, Earthquake Spectra, vol. 21, n.5, pp. 329-338

11 National Interagency Fire Center, http://www.nifc.gov/

12 Office of the Federal Coordinator for Meteorological Services and Supporting Research, *National Wildland Fire Weather: A Summary of User Needs and Issues*, Joint Action Group (JAG) for the National Wildland Fire Weather Needs Assessment (NWFWNA), 3 July 2007, p.2

13 U.S. Department of Agriculture Forest Service, *Federal Wildland Fire Policy*, Chartered 1994, Revised 2001. http://www.fs.fed.us/land/wdfire7c.htm, January 4, 2002

14 U.S. Fire Administration, TOPICAL FIRE RESEARCH SERIES, *Fires in the Wildland/Urban Interface*, Volume 2, Issue 16 March 2002

15 Interagency Working Group on Earth Observations, *Strategic Plan for the U.S. Integrated Earth Observation System*, Committee on Environment and Natural Resources, National Science and Technology Council, April 2005

16 The National Research Council, *Observing Weather and Climate From the Ground Up: A Nationwide Network of Networks*, The National Academies Press, Washington, DC, 2008 http://www.nap.edu/catalog.php?record_id=12540

17 National Institute of Medicine, Forum on Microbial Threats, *Global Climate Change and Extreme Weather Events: Understanding the Contributions to Infectious Disease Emergence* 2008, The National Academies Press, Washington, D.C., 2008; and National Institute of Medicine, Forum on Microbial Threats, *Vector-Borne Diseases: Understanding the Environmental, Human Health, and Ecological Connections*. The National Academies Press, Washington, D.C., 2008

18 Ocean's least productive waters are expanding, Polovina, J.J, E.A. Howell, and M. Abecassis, Geophysical Research Letters, vol. 35, L03618, doi:10.1029/2007GL031745, 2008

19   The United States National Report on Systematic Observations for Climate for 2008: National Activities with Respect to the Global Climate Observing System (GCOS) Implementation Plan, Prepared For Submission to the United Nations Framework Convention on Climate Change (UNFCCC), Compiled by the Observations Working Group of the U.S. Climate Change Science Program (CCSP), September 2008

20   L. Wigbels, G.R. Faith, and V. Sabathier, *Earth Observations and Global Change: Why? Where Are We? What's Next?*, Center for Strategic and International Studies, Washington DC, July 2008, pVII

21   Polovina, J.J., E.A. Howell, and M. Abecassis, *Ocean's least productive waters are expanding*, Geophysical Research Letters, Vol. 35, L03618, DOI:10.1029/2007GL031745, 2008

22   NSTC Subcommittee on Water Availability and Quality, *A Strategy for Federal Science and Technology to Support Water Availability and Quality in the United States*, National Science and Technology Council, Committee on Environment and Natural Resources, , Sept 2007, p.8

23   http://acwi.gov/monitoring/network/design/

www.ingramcontent.com/pod-product-compliance
Lightning Source LLC
Chambersburg PA
CBHW081242280526
45787CB00006B/2761